A PORTRAIT OF
SUSSEX

STEVE VIDLER
TEXT BY DIANA LEPPARD

Published by Heartwood Publishing
Bath, United Kingdom
www.heartwoodpublishing.co.uk

Photography by Steve Vidler

Text by Diana Leppard

Book design by Ian Gordon, Artstyle

Photographs and text copyright
Steve Vidler 2024

All rights reserved.
This book is sold subject to the condition that it shall not, by way of trade or otherwise, be lent, resold, hired out or otherwise circulated without Steve Vidler's prior written consent in any form of binding or cover other than that in which it is published and without a similar condition including this condition being imposed on the subsequent purchaser. No part of this publication may be reproduced, stored in a retrieval system or transmitted in any form or by any means, electronic and mechanical, photocopying, recording or otherwise without prior permission of Steve Vidler.

British Library Cataloguing in Publication Data

A catalogue record for this book is available
from the British Library.

ISBN 978 1 914515 95 8

Printed and bound in India by
Replika Press Pvt Ltd

A PORTRAIT OF
SUSSEX

DISCOVERING 1066 COUNTRY   14
A thousand years of life and landscape

FROM THE DOWNS TO THE SEA   68
Eastbourne, Lewes and the Bloomsbury Set

LA DOLCE VITA   132
Sun, scenery and celebration from Brighton to Chichester

LETTING OFF STEAM   198
Roaming the Rural Heartland

DISCOVERING 1066 COUNTRY

When dawn broke on the 14th of October 1066, it marked the beginning of a day that would change the face of Sussex, and of Anglo-Saxon England, forever. William, Duke of Normandy and his large invasion fleet had landed at Pevensey Bay just over two weeks earlier and were ready for battle. The English King, Harold Godwinson had been fighting in the North and many of his men remained there while he led others on the long march south to take on the new threat. It has been estimated that they walked around twenty-seven miles a day.

The Battle of Hastings began at 9am on the 14th of October and lasted just one day, but a day with much bloodshed. It ended with victory for the Normans. Harold was killed late in the battle and England had a new monarch, William the Conqueror, who was crowned on Christmas Day 1066.

Sussex not only had the site of the Battle of Hastings at its heart but also had ports that provided trade and transport links with France and so was affected more immediately and more significantly by the invasion than much of England. Its rich history and links to the battle are key to the county's enduring appeal. The eastern part of Sussex, which includes the towns of Battle, Hastings and Winchelsea and the countryside of the High Weald to the north, is known as 1066 Country and attracts visitors keen to explore its beautiful landscapes, historic buildings and fascinating culture.

Walkers can enjoy a thirty-one mile trail that starts by following the route taken by William and his forces to the battlefield. The 1066 Country Walk is a relatively easy, low-level route that begins at Pevensey Castle and passes Herstmonceux Castle before reaching the 1066 Battle Abbey and Battlefield site. It then heads to Winchelsea and ends in the town of Rye. Ten wooden sculptures by local artist, Keith Pettit that were partly inspired by the Bayeux Tapestry can be seen along the waymarked route, which passes through the High Weald Area of Outstanding Natural Beauty. Paths from Bexhill-on-Sea and Hastings link to the main trail and offer different access points and shorter route lengths.

After becoming King, one of William's most important tasks was to find out more about his new lands. He commissioned a great survey that was completed in 1086 and later became known as the Domesday Book. This record provides historians with important information about 11th century Sussex and gives fascinating details about the value of settlements before and after the invasion. Some of those in the vicinity of the battlefield were completely wasted and only recovered slowly over the following decades.

The 950th anniversary of the battle was marked in 2016 with a series of special events, a commemorative coin from the Royal Mint and newly created public art. The legacy of that fateful October day continues to resonate in 1066 Country.

Every year, on the October weekend nearest to the date of the Battle of Hastings, a re-enactment takes place on the original battlefield, which now forms the grounds of Battle Abbey. People travel from all over the world to take part in a reconstruction of the day that altered the course of history.

Although the Saxons used horses when travelling to battle, they fought on foot. The strongest section of Harold's army was the Housecarls, an infantry unit of paid, full-time soldiers who fought with two-handed axes. The Norman forces included around two thousand knights, who rode on horseback and carried swords, lances and shields. They were well-trained and many had experience of fighting within a tight-knit group. William's cavalry was a key factor in the outcome of the battle. Estimates of the total numbers involved in the fighting vary widely, but a figure of between five and seven thousand men per side has been suggested by recent research.

The re-enactment of the Battle of Hastings is organised by English Heritage. Although the event runs every year, with over three hundred re-enactors taking part, a larger version has been held every five years or so, involving as many as three thousand re-enactors and attracting an audience of many more. Some professional actors have been used more recently to help set the scenes, but the majority involved are amateur groups and enthusiasts.

The re-enactment is not just about the fighting but aims to immerse visitors in 11th century life, including the food, the clothes and the crafts. There are demonstrations of falconry and archery, and a camp where people can be seen working using traditional methods.

When William of Normandy invaded Britain, he made a vow that, if victory was his, a monastery would be founded. His forces won the battle, but at the expense of many lives and much bloodshed. To atone for this violence, William honoured the vow, and a Benedictine monastery was built on the battlefield. Battle Abbey *(left)* dates from around 1071 and is dedicated to the Trinity, the Virgin and St Martin of Tours. The high altar was placed over the spot where King Harold II was said to have fallen. Following the dissolution of the monasteries in the 16th century, Henry VIII gave the abbey and its lands to his friend, Sir Anthony Browne. Parts of the building were demolished, with the abbot's quarters being converted into a country house. Now under the care of English Heritage, the site is Grade I listed and opens to visitors throughout the year.

Above top: Chapter House glass displayed in the Great Gatehouse.

Above & left: The Great Gatehouse.

Prior to the Battle of Hastings in 1066, the area around the battlefield had been largely unpopulated but, following the foundation of the abbey, a settlement grew up around its boundaries. Now a town with a population of seven thousand, Battle sits in the High Weald Area of Outstanding Natural Beauty. The town still focuses on its association with William the Conqueror and some shops offer merchandise reflecting the link *(above left)*. The 1066 Sculpture by Guy Portelli was unveiled in 2016, to commemorate the 950th anniversary, and can be seen in the High Street *(above right)*.

Top left: Medieval timbered house in Battle. *Top right:* Battle Abbey. *Right:* Abbey Green & High Street, Battle.

The town of Rye sits at the confluence of three rivers and is now four miles inland from the sea. Old maps show that the coastline was very different in the Middle Ages when the settlement was at the top of a recessed bay that led off from the English Channel, which provided a safe haven for ships. A very attractive town, Rye is popular with visitors and has many historic buildings, including the Mermaid Inn *(left)*, whose cellars date from 1156. Rebuilt in 1420, the inn later became a haunt for smugglers, with a secret passageway, priest's hole and tales of ghosts.

Four fortified gateways were built early in the reign of Edward III to protect the routes into town. Only one of these still remains. Called the Landgate *(top right)*, it dates from 1329.

Top left: Mermaid Street. *Bottom left:* Small Lounge at the Mermaid Inn. *Bottom right:* Mermaid Inn sign.

The buildings in Rye show a fascinating mix of architectural styles. Mermaid Street has some fine examples of clapboard or weatherboard cottages *(above left)*, which are characteristic of Sussex. On the bottom corner of the street is the Old Borough Arms *(top left)*, which has the remains of the town wall as its base.

Ypres Tower *(right)* is one of the oldest buildings in Rye. It is thought to date from 1249, although actual construction may have been later. Used to defend against the French, it later became a prison, but is now part of the Rye Castle Museum. Exhibits within the tower include a replica of John Breads' skeleton with gibbet cage *(top right)* and a re-creation of a women's prison cell *(above right)*, as well as many other objects of local historical and archaeological interest. John Breads was convicted of murder in 1743.

On West Street in Rye stands Lamb House *(pp.32-33)*, a Georgian building that is in the care of the National Trust. The house was completed in 1722 for James Lamb and his family. A surprise royal visit took place a few years later; George I took refuge for the night when his ship washed ashore nearby. However, it is for its literary connections that Lamb House is particularly known. It has been home to many writers, notably Henry James and E F Benson. The house itself appeared as *'Mallards'* in Benson's Mapp & Lucia novels. Later tenants continued the literary and creative tradition and included the writer, Rumer Godden who lived here for seven years in the late 1960s, and Sir Brian Batsford-Cook who was a painter, designer and publisher. Lamb House is now a museum that celebrates the literary heritage of past residents.

The Parish Church of St Mary the Virgin (p.34) in Rye's Church Square is of particular architectural importance and is Grade I listed. The tower is open most of the year and a climb to the top offers a bird's eye view over the town to the countryside beyond (right). Inside the tower is one of the oldest church turret clocks still in working order. Made by Lewys Billiard, who was a Huguenot, it was installed in the 1560s. The church has eight bells (above), which weigh nearly 5 tons. The bells were stolen by looters in the 14th century and although later recovered, were recast and added to in the 1770s.

Winchelsea was founded in 1288 and replaced a previous settlement of the same name, which had been lost to the sea. The old town's population moved to the new site and the streets were laid out in a grid pattern, resulting in what is now one of England's best preserved planned towns from the medieval period. Three of the four town gates still stand, including Strand Gate *(left)*, which was built in the late 13th century and would have given access to the port. Historically an important port for the wine trade from Gascony, modern Winchelsea is known for its vineyards *(top right)* that produce a range of fine English wines.

Top left & above right: Parish Church of St Thomas the Martyr, with stained glass by Douglas Strachan (circa 1930).

The moated ruins of Bodiam Castle *(pp.38-39)* create a romantic scene, especially when the early morning mist rises from the water. This 14th century castle was originally built for Sir Edward Dallingridge and his wife. Although its likely role was to defend the area against possible French invasion during the Hundred Years War, it was built to impress and provided a luxury home for the family. Partially dismantled following the English Civil War, it became a picturesque ruin and was a fashionable place to visit in the 18th century, inspiring artists including JMW Turner. Early tourists left their mark, and the stones bear many examples of graffiti from this period. Bodiam Castle was left to the National Trust in 1925 and remains in their care today.

The Jacobean Wealden house, Bateman's (left) is famous as the home of writer and poet, Rudyard Kipling. In 1900, the Kiplings returned to England from America. Although the house was in a state of some disrepair, they were charmed by its sense of history and immediately felt that the 'Feng Shui' was good. It was a house they wanted to settle down in. Kipling was in his late 30s and a very famous author, so the privacy of the setting was also attractive. He bought Bateman's in 1902 and began a series of improvements, including the installation of a turbine at the mill, which generated electricity for the house. The grounds extend to 33 acres and were much loved by all the family. Kipling worked on designs to enhance the garden, including the planting of yew hedges and the addition of a rose garden.

Above: Rudyard Kipling by The Hon. John Collier (1891).

Rudyard Kipling died in 1936 and his wife, Carrie, lived another three years. Bateman's was left to the National Trust and so the interior has been retained as it was in their lifetime. The study (*p.43 top left*) was always an important part of the house, with Kipling continuing to write new works, including *Puck of Pook's Hill* which was inspired by the surrounding landscape. Kipling was awarded the Nobel Prize in Literature in 1907 and the citation (*p.43 top right*) forms part of a collection of over 4500 pieces that create a picture of his life and work.

Above: Sitting room. *P.43 bottom left:* Entrance to Bateman's. *P.43 bottom right:* Garden statue.

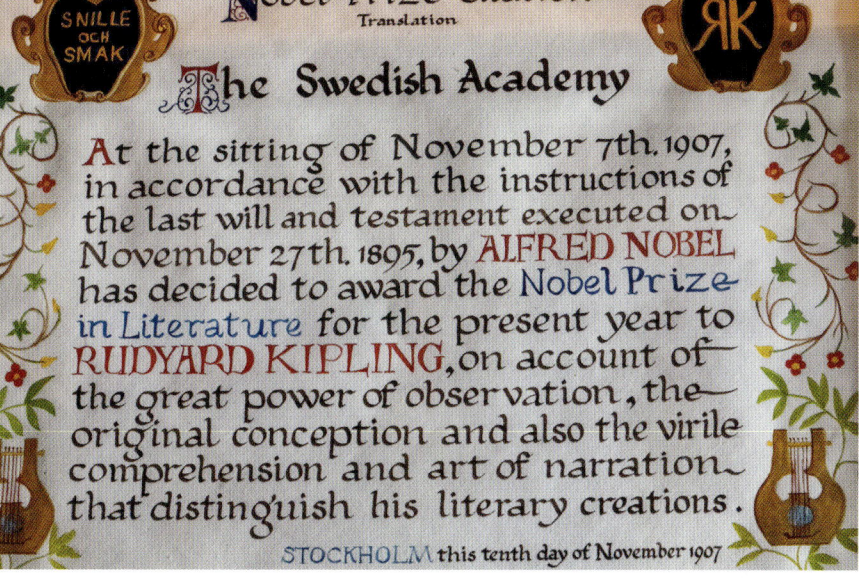

Hastings is a seaside town and fishing port whose picturesque Old Town sits in a sheltered valley between the sandstone cliffs of the East Hill and West Hill. The town's pier was originally designed by Victorian engineer, Eugenius Birch and opened in 1872. A popular attraction, it was at its prime in the 1930s, with more than fifty-five thousand people passing through the turnstiles in just one week in August 1931. After temporary closure during the war, the pier once again found its feet, becoming a centre for live music in the 1960s and 1970s. Bands who played in the pavilion included Jimi Hendrix, The Who, The Rolling Stones and Pink Floyd. Following a general decline and major storm damage, the pier eventually closed in 1999. Although restoration was planned, a disastrous fire in 2010 virtually destroyed the original buildings. The pier finally re-opened in 2016, as a sustainable, flexible platform *(above & top right)*. It was named 'Pier of the Year' in 2017 and also won the Stirling Prize for architecture.

Bottom right: The Landing by Leigh Dyer, commissioned to mark the 950th Anniversary of the Battle of Hastings in 2016.

The East Hill Lift *(above left)* is one of two funicular railways in Hastings. It has two cars, which can each take up to sixteen passengers and first opened in 1902. The line was converted to electricity and updated in the 1970s. A trip to the top offers fine views over Hastings Old Town *(right)* and also gives access to the Hastings Country Park. This nature reserve covers 853 acres and it is possible to see the French coast from the cliff top paths on a clear day.

Top: Rock-a-Nore Beach. *Above right:* Fishermen's Museum.

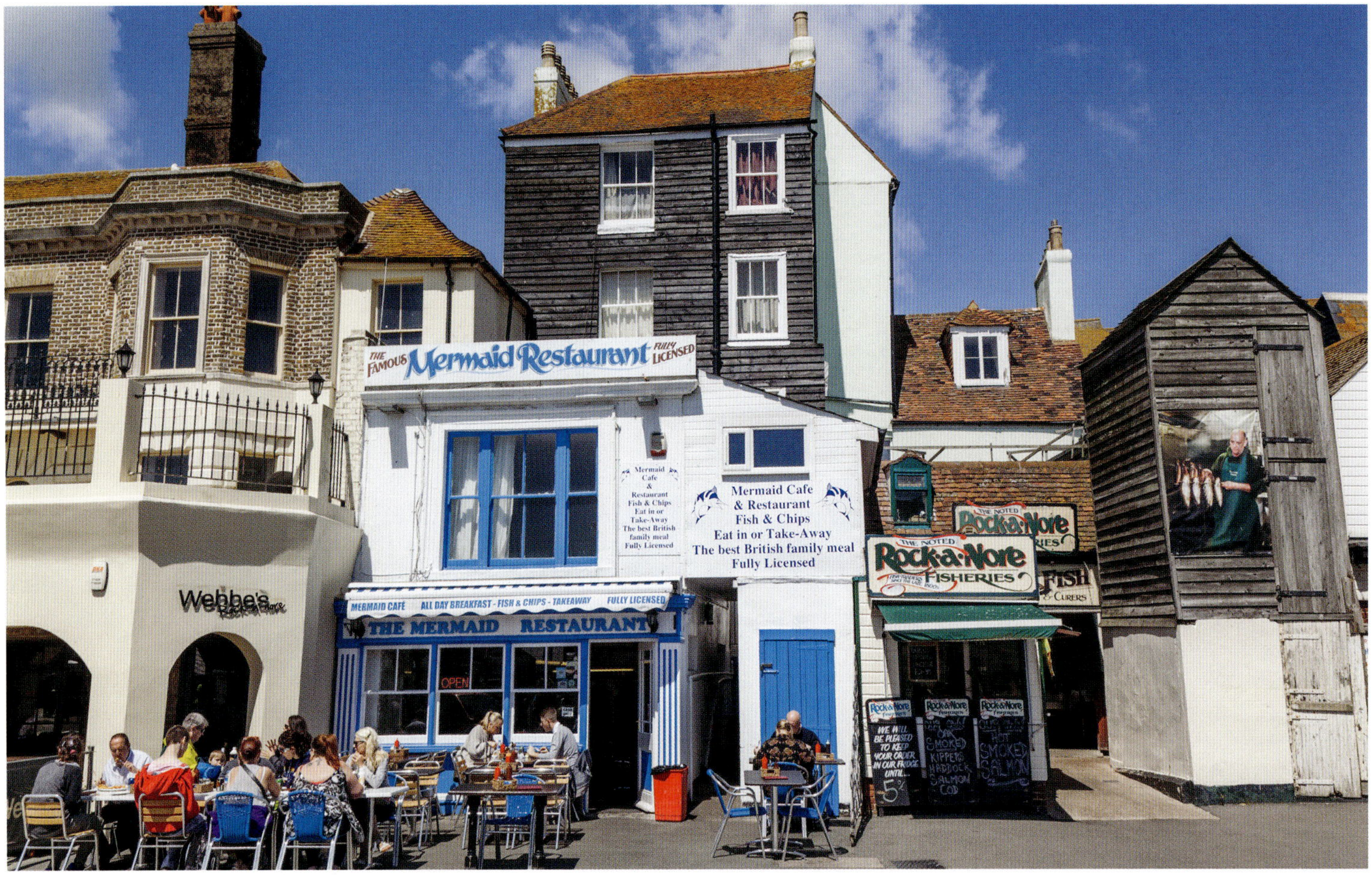
THE FAMOUS Mermaid Restaurant FULLY LICENSED
Mermaid Cafe
& Restaurant
Fish & Chips
Eat in or Take-Away
The best British family meal
Fully Licensed
THE MERMAID RESTAURANT
Rock-a-Nore
FISHERIES
Webbe's
OPEN

BUY NOW
COLLECT
LATER
DON'T MISS OUT!
OPEN TILL
4.30pm

PENBUCKLES
DELICATESSEN
MONMOUTH
COFFEE

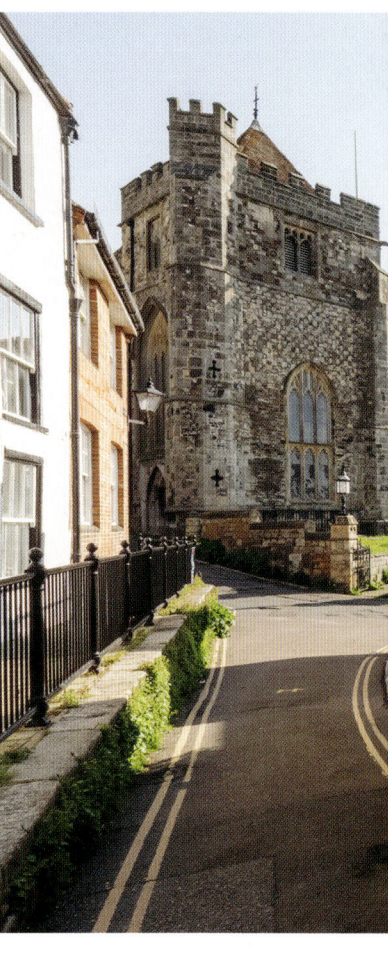

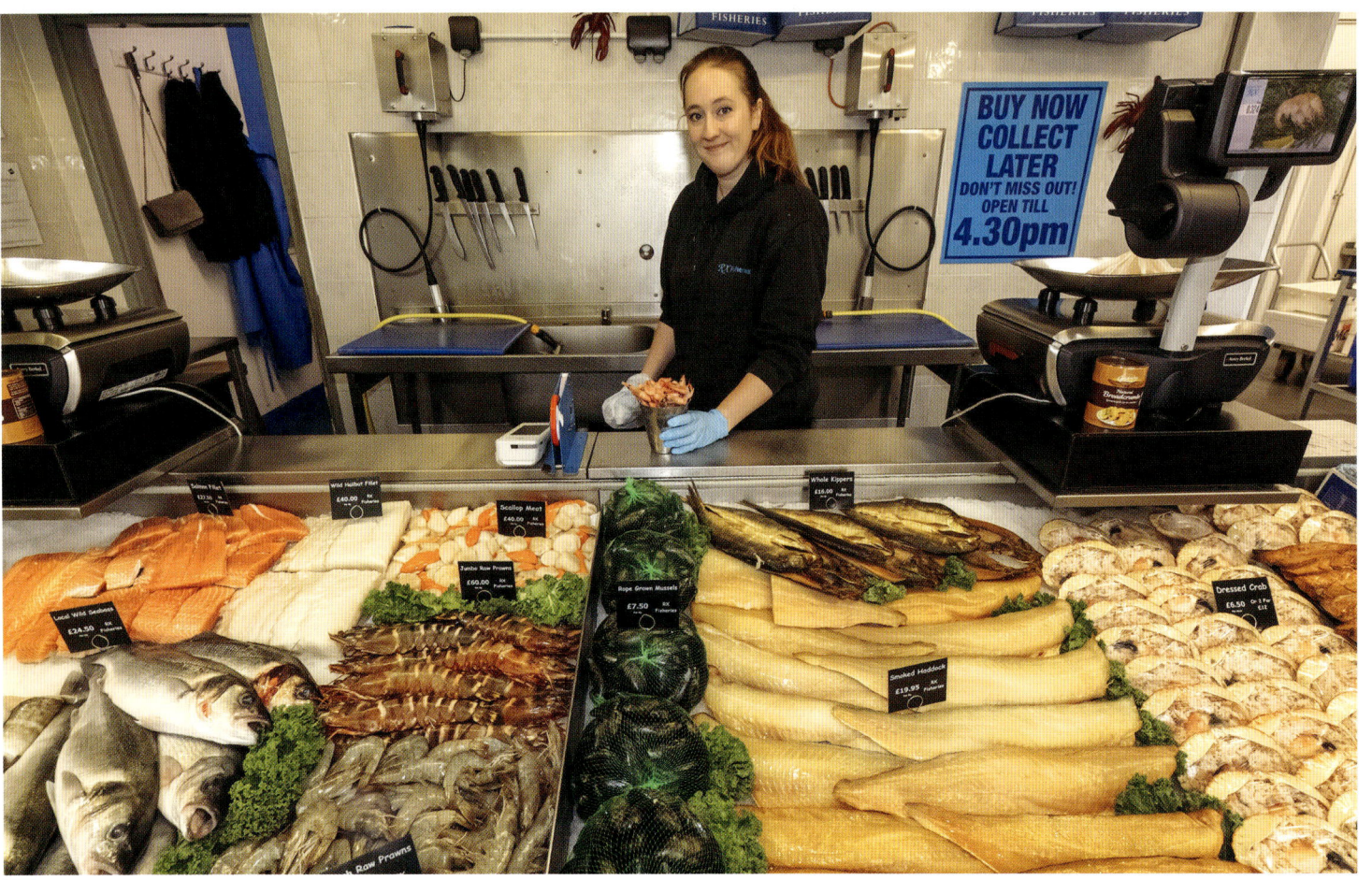

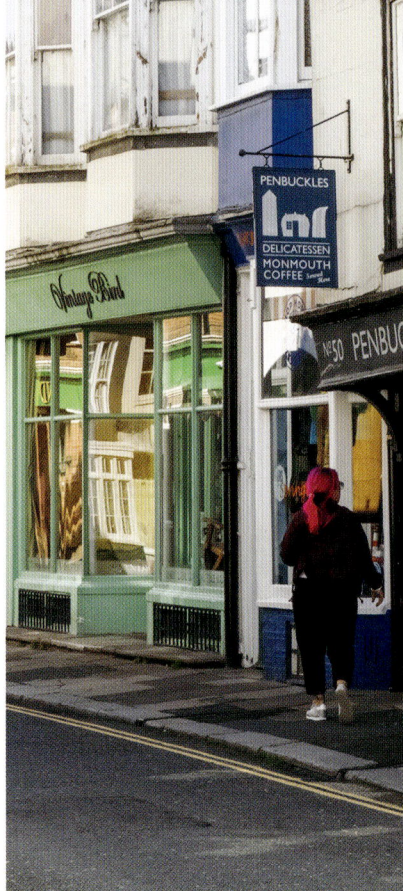

Hastings Old Town is a conservation area full of attractive buildings and independent shops that sell everything from food to antiques and bric-a-brac. George Street and the High Street *(bottom right)* are particularly popular with visitors. The area also has a huge selection of restaurants, cafes and bars, including the Mermaid on Rock-a-Nore Road *(top left)*, which is one of around fifty outlets in Hastings that specialise in the seaside favourite, fish & chips. A stone's throw from the Mermaid is RX Fisheries *(bottom left)*, which has been at the centre of the Old Town for more than seventy years and supplies fresh local fish caught using sustainable methods.

Top right: Hill Street & St Clement's Church.

Above: Motorcycle Rally on the seafront.

The shingle beach below the East Hill Lift in Hastings Old Town is called the Stade and Europe's biggest fleet of beach-launched fishing boats are based there *(above top)*. The net shops on the beach are a famous landmark in the town, with their distinctive colour and shape *(left & above)*. Built as protective stores for fishing gear in the mid-1830s, they were tarred and weatherboarded to make them waterproof. In the 19th century, the beach was not as large as it is today, and space was at a premium. The vertical design of the shops enabled a lot of gear to be stored on a small piece of land. They were originally built on posts, which enabled the sea to flow beneath them, but in later years, the shingle built-up and the water no longer reaches.

Next to the Fishermen's Museum on Rock-a-Nore Road is Hastings Aquarium. There are a number of different sections in the building, including the Native Zone, which focuses on species living in the UK; the Nursery, with its breeding tanks; the Ray Tank and Rivers & Estuaries, which has freshwater species from South Asia, including archerfish and turtles. The Jungle Room is home to many different species of reptile, with the green tree python from Papua New Guinea *(above)* & the Argentine Tegu Lizard *(left)* amongst the species that can be seen.

The highlight of the aquarium is an underwater tunnel, which runs through the Ocean Tank and enables visitors to walk beneath a host of tropical species, including blacktip reef sharks *(left)* and rays. Black tip reef sharks average 1.6 metres in length and are found in the coral reefs of the Indian and Pacific Oceans. Slightly smaller, is the longhorn cowfish *(below)*, which lives in the same habitat but only reaches a maximum length of fifty centimetres.

Not for the faint-hearted, the True Crime Museum in Hastings tells tales of gangsters, poisoners, forensics and more. Exhibits focus on some of the world's most notorious criminals, including the acid bath murderer, John Haigh *(right)*, whose actions in the 1940s were the subject of the television film, A is for Acid, which starred Martin Clunes in the lead role. Also on display is a double-decker coffin *(left)* of the type used by Italian-American crime boss, Joseph Bonanno during his reign as head of the family from 1931 until the late 1960s. Amongst his many business interests was a funeral parlour in Brooklyn, which was thought to be a front for the disposal of bodies. The design of the coffin allowed two bodies to be buried in one grave.

P.54 Bottom left: The story of Mexican drug lord, Zeta 3 - Heriberto Lazcano.

P.54 Bottom right: Display of handcuffs, leg fetters and other restraints.

Hastings Traditional Jack in the Green is a festival that takes place every year to celebrate May Day and to welcome summer. Held over four days, it attracts thousands of visitors who come to the town to enjoy the atmosphere, listen to live bands and join in the dancing. The main procession takes place on the Bank Holiday Monday, when everything goes green. The giant Jack *(p.59 bottom left)*, who is covered with foliage, is led through the Old Town and up to West Hill, where he is finally 'slain', so releasing the spirit of summer for another year.

The Jack in the Green tradition is thought to date from the 18th century, although it evolved from earlier celebrations of May Day. By the early 20th century, the tradition had died out across the country but was revived in Hastings in 1983 by Mad Jack's Morris, a local group of morris dancers now called Hastings RX Morris. Teams of dancers, known as 'sides', and folk musicians travel to the town from all over the country and beyond to take part in the festivities.

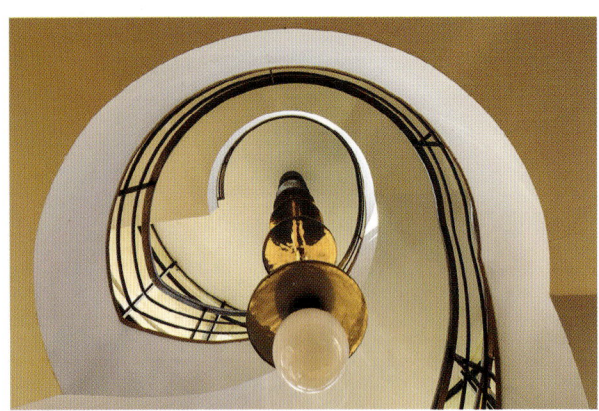

The De La Warr Pavilion *(pp.60-61)* is the jewel in the crown of Bexhill-on-Sea. This iconic building on the seafront dates from 1935 and is a Grade I listed building. A fine example of Modernist architecture, it was built as an entertainment hall and opened by the then Duke and Duchess of York (later King George VI and Queen Elizabeth). During the Second World War it was taken over by the army to defend against possible German invasion; comedian Spike Milligan was one of the soldiers who were stationed here. The Pavilion lacked maintenance in the 1970s and became rundown, but a full restoration project took place in the 21st century, with the Pavilion re-opening as a contemporary arts centre in 2005.

The village of Pevensey lies just inland from Pevensey Bay, forever renowned as the landing point for William the Conqueror and his forces in 1066. The medieval castle ruins seen at Pevensey today are on the site of a Roman 'Saxon Shore' fort, where the Normans stayed before the Battle of Hastings. The fort subsequently remained of considerable strategic importance to them, and a castle with a stone keep and bailey was built within the Roman walls. This remained in use until the late 16th century, after which it fell into decay. Now in the care of English Heritage, Pevensey Castle *(left & above)* is open to visitors, who can explore its history reaching back over seventeen hundred years to the 4th century.

Below: The Swan Fish & Chips, Pevensey.

Set within beautiful East Sussex countryside, the 15th century castle of Herstmonceux *(right)* is one of the oldest brick-built buildings in England. The castle was dismantled and became a picturesque ruin in the 18th century but was comprehensively restored and turned into a residence between 1913 and the early 1930s. More recently, it has been used as a study centre for Queen's University in Canada. The moated castle is surrounded by 300 acres of formal gardens and parkland, with themed gardens including the Shakespeare, Elizabethan and Apothecary. The romantic setting makes it a popular venue for weddings *(above)* and other weekend events.

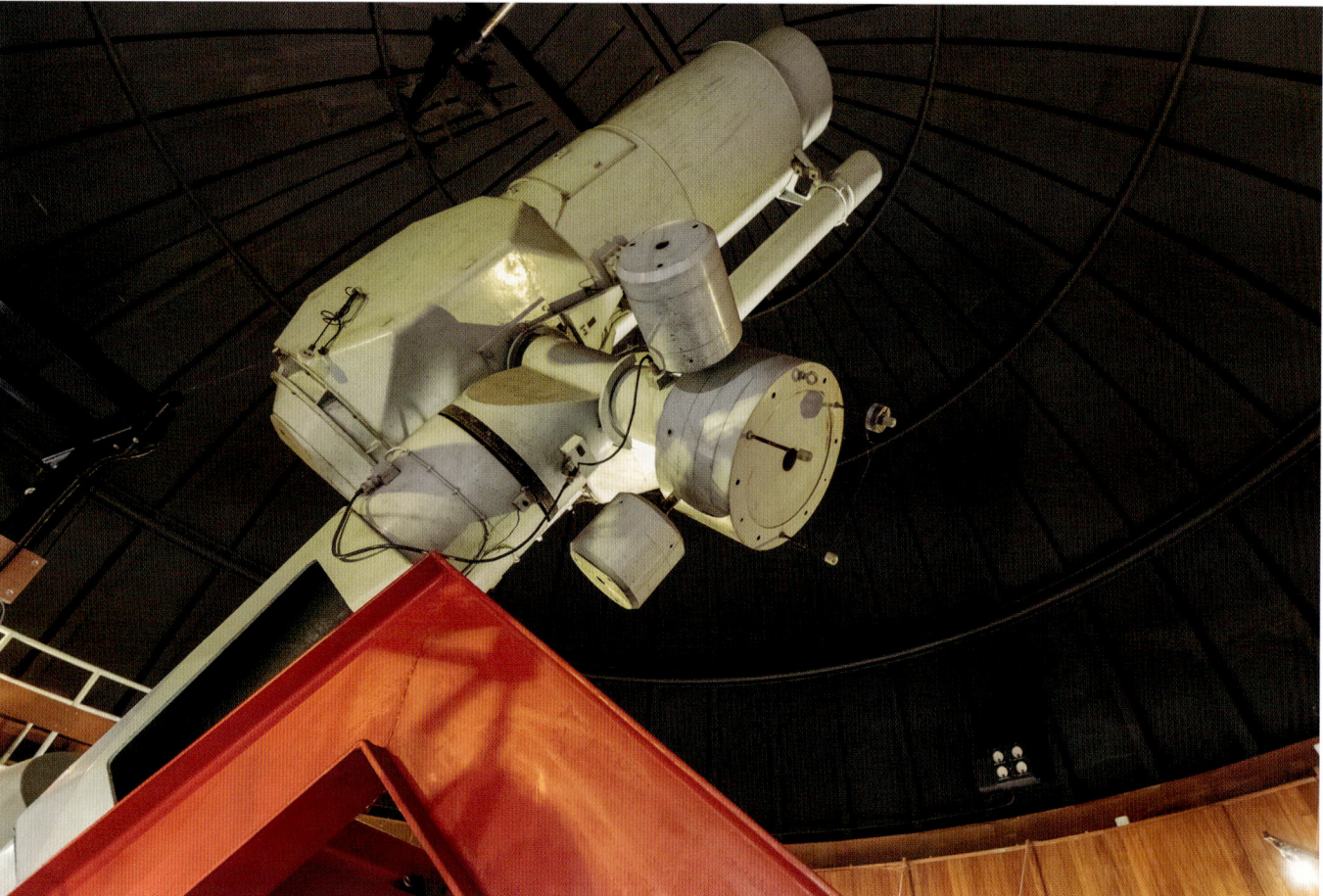

Charles II founded the Royal Greenwich Observatory in London in 1675 but, by the mid-20th century, light pollution had become a problem. In 1948, the move began and nine years later the Royal Greenwich Observatory at Herstmonceux had been established within the castle grounds. It stayed here until 1988, when it relocated to Cambridge. Some telescopes remain *(above & middle left)*, although the largest was moved out in the 1970s. Known as the Isaac Newton telescope, its dome is still a distinctive landmark at the site. The buildings *(top left & right)* are now an educational resource for schoolchildren and have been renamed as the Observatory Science Centre.

Right: John Flamsteed, the first Astronomer Royal.

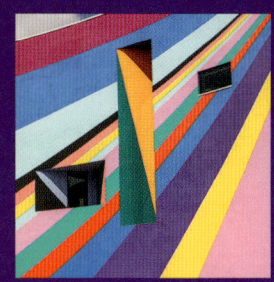

FROM THE DOWNS TO THE SEA

The story of Sussex begins many centuries before the Norman Conquest. The county name derives from the Old English, Suth-Seaxe meaning the land of the South Saxons, who came over from Germany to settle in the region in the fifth and sixth centuries. Their Anglo-Saxon kingdom was conquered by Wessex in the 9th century and soon became part of the newly-formed kingdom of England. Its roots, however, stretch much further back in time and important vestiges of both Iron Age and Roman occupation can be found within the county's boundaries.

The beautiful downland landscape was designated as a National Park in 2010 and more than two-thirds of the South Downs National Park lies within Sussex, reaching down to England's southern coastline at one of the country's most iconic landscapes, the Seven Sisters chalk cliffs with their highest point of Beachy Head. The chalk platforms and subtidal ridges at the base of the cliffs are amongst the most important marine chalk habitats in the south-east and are home to rare and threatened species of wildlife, including blue mussels, native oysters and the short-snouted seahorse.

The county was divided into two parts for administrative purposes in the 1970s and the ceremonial counties of East and West Sussex were formed, each with its own county town and local government. However, the spirit of the united county is still strong, and Sussex is generally recognised and marketed as one cultural region offering many unique attractions.

On the 16th of June every year, Sussex Day is celebrated. This was introduced in 2007 to highlight the rich heritage and culture found across the county.

Sussex also has a flag, which is based on a traditional emblem. It was only registered in 2011, but its roots are much older. The flag depicts six gold martlets on a blue ground. Martlets are mythical birds that are said to stay on the wing and never settle. They symbolise continuous effort and represent the six historic Rapes, or sub-divisions, of the county.

More than 1.5 million people live in the 1461 square miles of Sussex. Its southern boundary stretches along the English Channel coast for 140 miles and is a magnet for the many millions of tourists who visit annually – a figure that reached a record of more than 60 million in the recent past.

Visitors over the decades have enjoyed the varied entertainment provided by the traditional seaside pier, particularly after the advent of the railways that brought the scenic coastline within easy reach of England's capital. Most piers have chequered pasts, with storms, fires and the rise of cheap, overseas package holidays just a few of the factors threatening their existence. St Leonard's Pier in Hastings and the West Pier in Brighton are amongst those that found the struggle too great, but other historic piers continue to stand along the Sussex coast as testament to their enduring appeal and the ingenuity of those who built them.

With a resident population of 100,000, the seaside resort of Eastbourne is already a large town on England's south coast, but it also attracts around five million visitors each year, who travel down to soak up the sun and enjoy a stroll along the seafront. Known as the sunniest place in the UK, it has a unique position at the base of the South Downs and by the cliffs of Beachy Head. The town was developed into a fashionable resort in the Victorian era, largely thanks to William Cavendish, later the 7th Duke of Devonshire, who was one of two primary landowners. In the mid-19th century, he commissioned a plan for the development of a large resort from the architect, Henry Currey. The idea of a pier was viewed favourably by Cavendish and although there were delays in its construction, it finally opened in the early 1870s *(above & pp.72-73)*.

Top & left: Beach huts on Eastbourne seafront.

As with many seaside piers, the one at Eastbourne has had a chequered history since first opening more than 150 years ago; with fires, storms and damage by a wartime mine only a few of the challenges it has faced. Just five years after opening, the section nearest to the shore was washed away and had to be rebuilt. Later, during the Second World War, parts of the decking were taken away and machine guns were installed as defensive measures against invasion.

Now fully restored following a catastrophic fire in 2014, Eastbourne Pier offers a new walkway, with shops, eating places, entertainment venues *(above)* and beautiful views of the English Channel *(right)*. The highest point of the pier, some 40 metres above sea level, is the golden dome *(top right)*. Reached by the Triumphal Staircase, this dome houses a camera obscura, which dates from around 1900.

The shingle beach at Eastbourne is protected by wooden breakwaters or groynes, which are a distinctive feature of seafront views of the town *(right)*. There are ninety-four in all, along a five-mile stretch of coast. These are essential to prevent erosion and were first installed in the late 1800s. Constantly pummelled by waves, they need to be maintained and replaced on a regular basis and their size was increased in the early 1990s. The groynes are now made of Greenheart timber from Guyana, which is very durable and resistant to rot.

Above: Eastbourne Pier at dawn.

William Cavendish's vision for Eastbourne in the 19th century resulted in the construction of many fine Victorian buildings, which still grace the seafront today. The Grand Hotel *(left)* on King Edward's Parade was built in 1875. Also known as the White Palace, its impressive frontage overlooks the beach. Many famous people have stayed within its walls, with past guests including Winston Churchill, Arthur Conan Doyle and the composers, Elgar and Debussy.

Above: Along the seafront.

Eastbourne has much to offer the cultural visitor, with a choice of theatres, galleries and other entertainment spaces. Theatres include the Congress, the Devonshire Park *(above)*, the Winter Garden and the Royal Hippodrome *(above middle)*, all offering ongoing programmes of plays, musicals, comedy and opera. The Stage Door pub *(above top)* is popular with theatregoers.

Towner Eastbourne *(right & p.69)* is an award-winning contemporary art space that offers changing exhibitions by famous names from around the world. The gallery first opened to the public in 1923 but moved to its newly-built, current premises in 2009. The exterior mural was added in 2019. Called *Dance Diagonal,* it was designed by German artist, Lothar Götz.

The Royal Hippodrome *(left)* is the oldest theatre in Eastbourne and dates from 1883. An important part of the community, the theatre not only plays host to a full range of professional productions, but also encourages local drama and school groups. A restoration project in 2023 updated the décor and replaced seating.

On the seafront is Eastbourne Bandstand *(above)*, which calls itself the 'Busiest Bandstand on Planet Earth'. Built in 1935, it is flanked by a colonnade and viewing decks. A popular music venue, it attracts large audiences who sit in the open air to enjoy the entertainment.

Another institution that owes its origins to William Cavendish is Eastbourne College *(above)*, a fee-paying school that was founded in 1867. When the town's doctor and other prominent local citizens decided that an independent school was required, Cavendish supported the project and supplied land at a reasonable price. Originally only providing education for boys, the college started to accept girls in 1968 and was fully co-educational by 1995.

Left: Stained glass windows in Eastbourne College Chapel.

Eastbourne also hosts a number of cultural events, festivals and fairs throughout the year. In addition to the International Airshow, which attracts thousands of visitors annually, recent festivals have been dedicated to the performing arts, steampunk, film, food and music. The Eastbourne Carnival *(left & above)* is one of the biggest of its kind in South East England, with around fifteen hundred people taking part and many more watching the fun from the sidelines. Local dance and fitness groups, including the Cherry Dance company *(left)* who have appeared on *Britain's Got Talent*, perform alongside Latin American dancers *(above top)* who travel to the town for the day.

Another visually exciting event held annually in Eastbourne is the Bonfire Society Procession & Fireworks *(pp.68, 90 & 91)*, which is held on the seafront in Autumn. The procession starts at the Crown & Anchor pub on Royal Parade and heads up to the RNLI Lifeboat Station. The evening ends with a bonfire on the beach and an impressive firework display. Sussex towns and villages are known for their fire festivals, with the nearby town of Lewes being home to the most celebrated, which is always held on the 5th of November.

One of England's finest and most recognisable views is that of the Seven Sisters chalk cliffs, which border the English Channel and run from Cuckmere Haven along to the outskirts of Eastbourne *(left & above)*. Walkers can enjoy a path that runs the full length of the cliffs. Although the undulations make this a journey of more than twenty-one kilometres, it is technically easy and well worth the effort for the stunning coastal scenery and varied natural landscape that it offers. The highest of the cliffs is Beachy Head *(above top)*, which stands 162 metres above sea level.

The main access point to the beach below the Seven Sisters is at Birling Gap *(pp.94-95)*. Erosion by the sea and by rainwater causes ongoing changes in the cliffs and makes the landscape very fragile. The cliffs can erode as much as a metre in a year, leaving behind distinctive chalk platforms. Bad storms in 2014 led to an erosion rate, in a two-month period, usually seen over seven years. Rock falls are a regular feature and it is possible to be cut off by the tides, so care must be taken, but the intriguing rock pools and low-level views of the cliffs make this a popular location.

The South Downs National Park is the newest member of England's National Park family. It covers more than 1600 square miles and is home to many important natural habitats, including the Seven Sisters coastline.. The area manages to retain its beauty despite being located at the centre of one of Britain's most populated areas and plays host to millions of visitors each year. The cliffs are regular stars of the big and small screen, appearing in films such as *Atonement, Fantastic Beasts* and *Robin Hood: Prince of Thieves*.

Just north of Birling Gap is the village of East Dean, home to the Tiger Inn *(right)*. The unusual name may derive from the coat of arms of a local landowner, which actually depicted leopards, but people were not familiar with the characteristics of different big cats at the time. Whatever the reason, the inn's location by the village green makes it an ideal stopping place. Devotees of Sir Arthur Conan Doyle will know that his famous fictional detective, Sherlock Holmes, retired to a Sussex village and a few clues suggest East Dean may have been the place; a blue plaque celebrates this link *(above middle)*.

Above top: the meanders of the River Cuckmere.

Above: Cottage in East Dean.

In the valley of the River Cuckmere is the village of Alfriston, which nestles around a village green called the Tye. St Andrew's Church *(above middle)* sits at its centre and dates primarily from the 14th century, but with earlier origins. Its large size and elevated position have led to this parish church being known as the 'Cathedral of the Downs' and it features on the newer of the two village signs *(left)*. In 1931, author and poet, Eleanor Farjeon used Alfriston as inspiration when writing her hymn, *Morning Has Broken*, later made famous by Cat Stevens.

Above top & above: Alfriston village stores.

Beside the church in Alfriston sits the 14th century Clergy House *(pp.102-103)*, which is of particular significance as it was the first property acquired by the National Trust in 1896 and remains in their care to this day. The hall at the centre of the property became the first room that they ever opened to the public. An example of a Wealden hall house, the medieval building has a timber frame and structure particularly found in East Sussex and Kent. Different rooms in the house have now been set up to reflect the time periods of former residents and to tell their fascinating stories.

In a picturesque setting, on an island surrounded by the River Cuckmere, is the Tudor building of Michelham Priory. The island was formerly home to an Augustinian Priory, dating back to the 13th century, but this was seized in 1537 and partially destroyed during the dissolution of the monasteries; the west wing was subsequently added. The property provided a home for evacuees and a base for the Canadian Army in World War II and is now cared for by the Sussex Archaeological Society. The grounds cover more than seven acres and include physic and medieval herb gardens.

Left: Exterior view. *Above (clockwise from top left):* Window (1967) in Prior's Room based on seal of Prior John Leem; main staircase; spinning demonstration.

On the slopes of Windover Hill, above the village of Wilmington, stands the distinctive chalk outline of the Long Man of Wilmington *(far right)*. There are more than fifty hill figures in Britain, but this is the largest that takes human form. At nearly seventy metres tall, the man has been carved to look in proportion when viewed from below. Originally thought to date back many centuries, improved research methods now suggest that it may be more recent – possibly 400 to 500 years old. Whatever the historical truth, the Long Man now stands as an impressive guardian to the rolling landscape of the South Downs *(right)*.

Above: Middle Farm Shop at Firle.

The coastal town of Seaford sits at the western end of the Seven Sisters cliffs and was an important port in the Middle Ages. The following centuries saw a gradual decline and it wasn't until the railway arrived in the 19th century that fortunes improved, with Seaford becoming popular as a small resort. The beach *(above right)* is the main attraction, being a broad sweep of sand and shingle. At the eastern end of the esplanade is a Martello tower *(left)*, one of a number of small defensive forts built across the British Empire in the first half of the 19th century. Numbered 74, it is now home to the Seaford Museum.

Top and above left: Runners on Seaford seafront

Within the Martello tower at Seaford is the Seaford Museum, whose collection spans a period from prehistoric times to the present day. The compact exterior of the tower is deceptive, as the museum has a display area exceeding 450 square metres, which includes the roof area and the covered dry moat.

Focusing on the history of the local area, Seaford Museum was established in 1979. Built around 1808, the interior of the tower *(left)* provides a unique setting for a range of informative tableaux and exhibitions, including reconstructions of shops and domestic rooms from different time periods *(above top right)* and ships' figureheads *(above right)*.

Above top left: Stained glass from St Peter's School Chapel. *Above left:* Rooftop cannon.

At the heart of the South Downs National Park is Charleston (left & above), a farmhouse that is famous for its association with a creative group of artists, writers and intellectuals who mainly lived in the first half of the 20th century. Members included writer, Virginia Woolf and her sister, the artist Vanessa Bell, as well as John Maynard Keynes, Duncan Grant, Clive Bell and Lytton Strachey. Collectively known as the Bloomsbury Group, they used to live, work or study in the Bloomsbury area of London. Clive Bell married Vanessa in 1907, and although the marriage had largely failed by the outbreak of war, they never divorced. From 1916, Charleston became the country home of Vanessa, her two sons and artist Duncan Grant, but it was also an important rural retreat for others in the group.

The Bloomsbury Group has become known for the complicated relationships between its members. Although Vanessa lived at Charleston with fellow artist, Duncan Grant, her husband frequently visited, sometimes accompanied by his mistress. Vanessa and Duncan lived and worked together for four decades, and had a daughter, Angelica, who was raised as Clive Bell's own. Grant was primarily homosexual and his lover, David Garnett, also lived at the farmhouse. The decorative interior is a testament to the creativity of the group's art *(above & right)*.

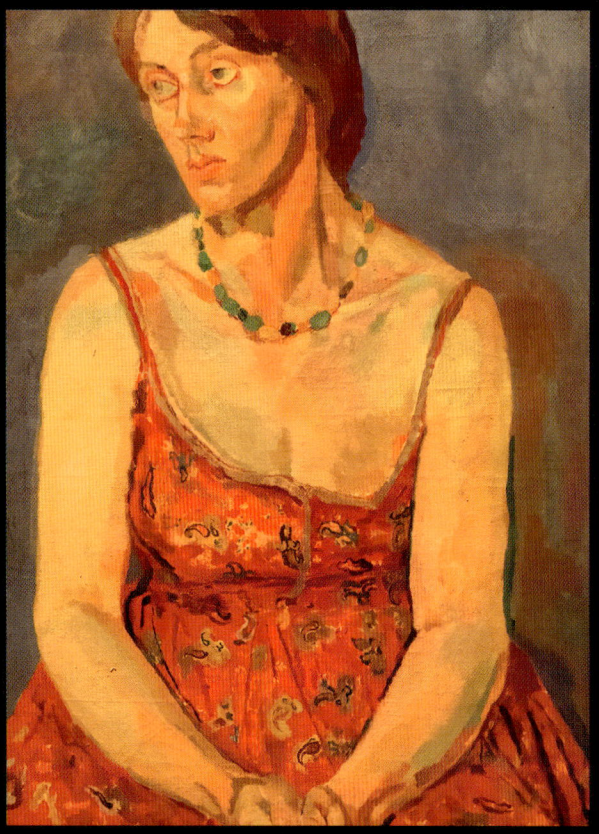

Charleston now opens to the public and contains furniture, painting and objects that demonstrate the artistic styles of the Bloomsbury Group within a domestic context. A number of exhibitions and special events take place throughout the year, including a literary festival each May.

Top left: Edward Le Bas (Self-portrait 1949).   *Above middle:* Vanessa Bell by Duncan Grant (c.1918) *Top right:* Duncan Grant (Self-portrait 1965). *Other:* Famous Women Dinner Plates (from a collection of 50, hand-decorated by Vanessa Bell & Duncan Grant).   *Right:* The Studio at Charleston.

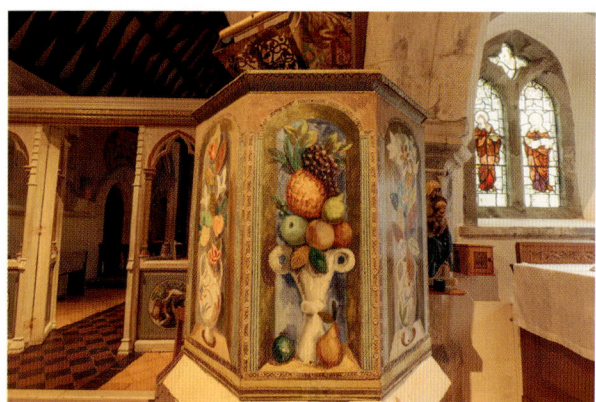

Three miles south-east of Charleston, in the village of Berwick, stands the church of St Michael & All Angels, which has further fine examples of paintings by the Bloomsbury Group. The church interior is comprehensively decorated with murals created by Duncan Grant, Vanessa Bell and her son, Quentin. They were commissioned in 1941 by Bishop Bell of Chichester, who hoped to help re-introduce the artistic tradition that had been lost after the Reformation. The initial proposals for the design were put forward by Duncan Grant, who was the lead artist for the project. He and Vanessa wanted all the paintings to work together, making a decorative scheme, rather than just being viewed as separate entities.

THE HOPE INN
MEET · EAT · DRINK

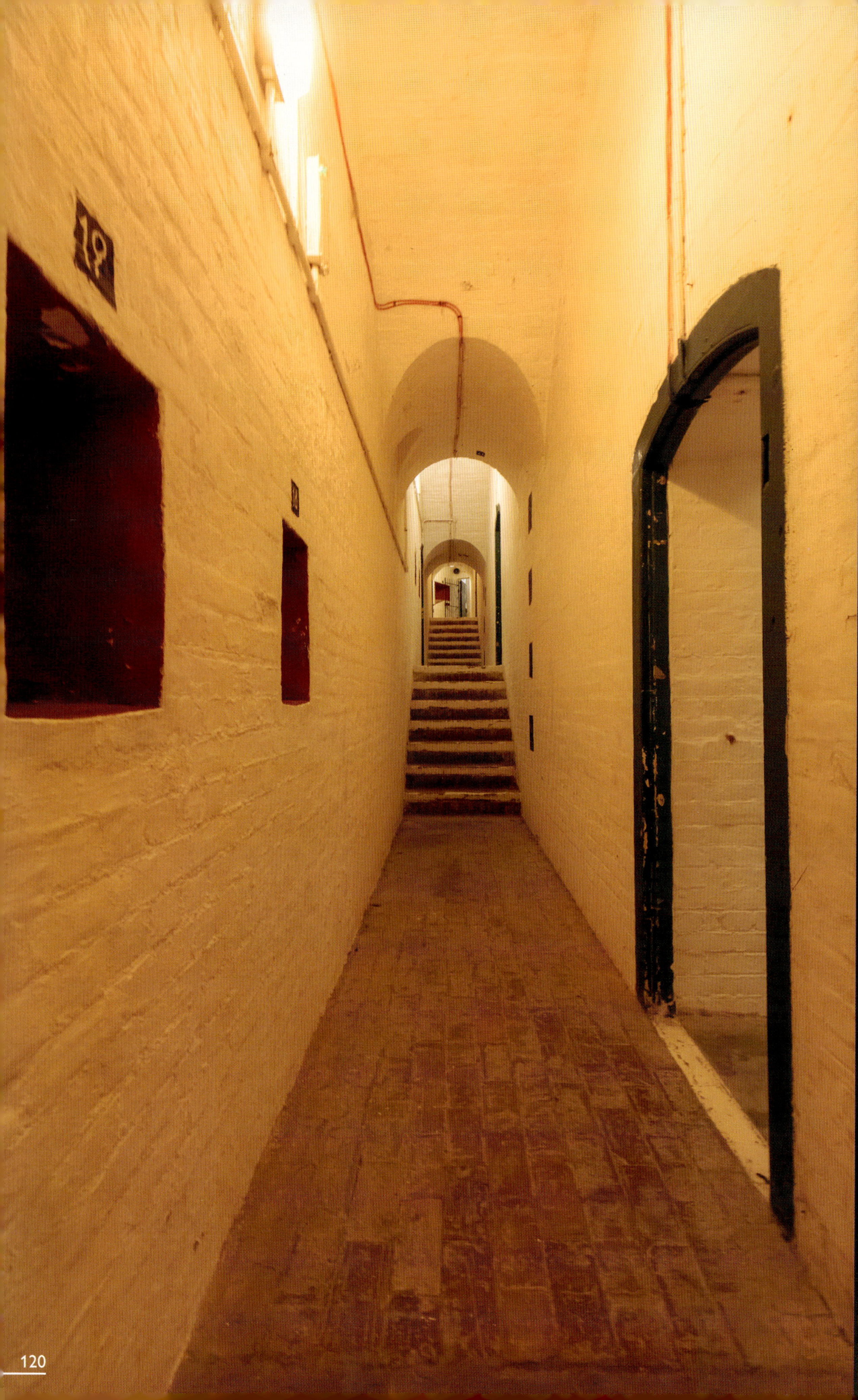

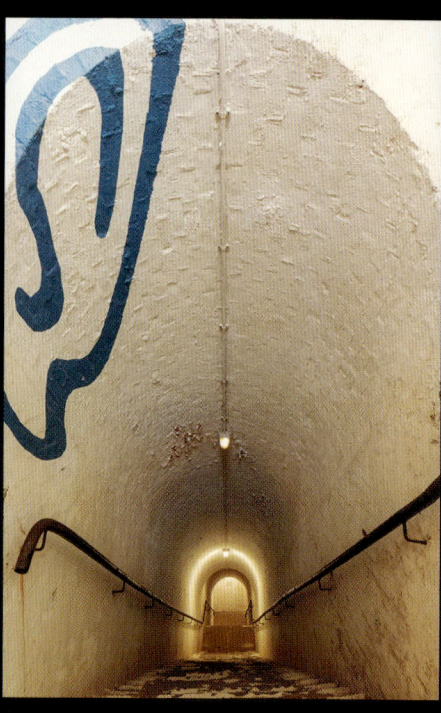

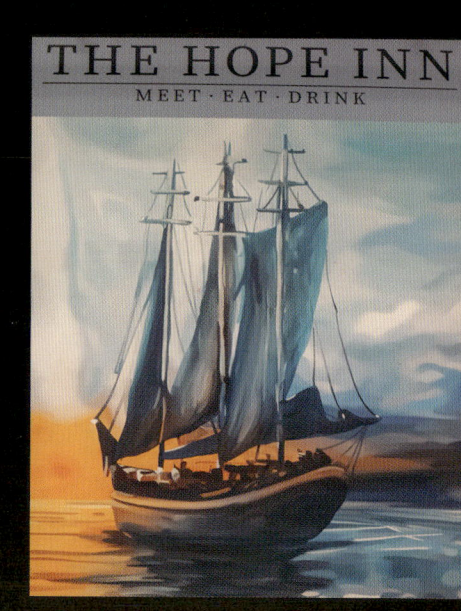

During the medieval period, the busy port at Seaford began to silt up, and an alternative was needed so that easy access to the sea could be maintained. The mouth of the River Ouse, a few miles to the west, was the chosen location. The new harbour, or Newhaven, was built in the mid-1500s, with a breakwater added by the end of the 18th century. The town is still important as a cross channel terminal *(right)*, with a regular schedule of passenger and freight services. On the west side of the harbour is Newhaven Fort *(below and left)*, built in the 19th century to defend the harbour. Now open as a museum, it is the largest defence structure in Sussex, taking nearly ten years to complete and using an estimated six million bricks.

P.120 bottom: The Hope Inn on Fort Road.

Lewes is traditionally seen as the county town of Sussex, and the castle holds a commanding position at its heart. Originally constructed soon after the Battle of Hastings, this Norman castle guarded the River Ouse, whose valley provided an access point to the South Downs and beyond. The mound on which it stands was man-made and the structure is unusual. It is a motte-and-bailey castle, but this design traditionally has one tower of stone or wood on top of a mound that is surrounded by a bailey, or walled courtyard. Lewes and Lincoln are the only castles in England to have two mottes. Those at Lewes are known as Brack Mount and The Keep, and a climb to the top of The Keep is rewarded with panoramic views across the surrounding countryside. Adjoining the castle is Barbican House, home to the Museum of Sussex Archaeology, whose collection showcases the history of the county from prehistoric times through to the Middle Ages.

Lewes is a traditional market town, with a range of historic buildings and independent shops that make it very attractive to visitors. The Fifteenth Century Bookshop is at Number 99 on the High Street *(right)* and has had the same owner since 1986. At the junction of the High Street and Market Street stands the war memorial *(above middle)*, which was designed by the sculptor, Vernon March. This commemorates the local men who perished in both World Wars and is topped by a statue of Victory, standing on a globe and holding up a laurel wreath. Peace and Liberty sit at the base.

Top: White Hart Hotel.

Above: H. A. Baker Ltd Pharmacy, 44 High Street.

The 15th century Bull House *(left)* stands at the western end of Lewes High Street and was once home to writer and revolutionary, Thomas Paine. Born in England in 1737, he was a political writer and pamphleteer who later moved to America and played a significant role in the American War of Independence. Lewes is also the base of Harvey's Brewery *(above right)*, and a summer walk around the town through the little alleyways or twittens may well end up raising a thirst. *Above:* Lewes town views.

Lewes is a haven for those who love browsing in antique and vintage shops, with a number of emporiums to discover in the town centre. Based in an old Methodist chapel, the Flea Market on Market Street is open seven days a week and has a range of eclectic stalls with a wide selection of items on display. This is only one of many choices, another being the Lewes Antiques Centre on Cliffe High Street, which has five floors to explore and more than eighty vendors to visit.

A few miles outside Lewes, in the village of Rodwell, is Monk's House *(top left)*. This weatherboarded cottage was once the summer retreat of the writers, Virgina Woolf and her husband Leonard. Like Charleston, the cottage played an important part in the lives of the Bloomsbury Group. Now cared for by the National Trust, this 17th century cottage had a succession of owners before being bought at auction by the Woolf's in 1919 for the sum of £700. They lived here until their deaths, ending with Leonard's death fifty years later in 1969. A portrait of Virginia as a young woman *(above)*, by her sister Vanessa Bell, hangs in the dining room.

Bottom left: Living room.
Below: Virginia Woolf's bedroom.

On the south side of Lewes town centre is Anne of Cleves House *(above & far left)*, named after the fourth wife of Henry VIII. Following her short-lived marriage to the monarch, Anne was granted a number of properties, of which this was one. Although she never actually lived here, the timber-framed Wealden house, which dates back to the 15th century is now a museum that gives visitors an idea of what life would have been like in Anne's time. The interiors are well-preserved and include a Tudor kitchen, parlour and bedroom with a four-poster bed *(left)*. The garden is also based on a planting scheme from the period.

LA DOLCE VITA

Most of the people who make Sussex their home live along the coastal band, with the largest concentration by far in Brighton and the surrounding area. Around a third of the county's population is found within the metropolitan area and residents enjoy the benefits of coastal living but also have easy access to London via rail. Brighton has developed a reputation for being one of the 'coolest' cities in Britain and has long been a draw for hipsters and others working in the creative industries.

The London and Brighton Railway was completed in 1841 and with it came dramatic change. Visitors from London were able to make the journey without committing to an overnight stay and so the era of the day-tripper began. This influx needed entertainment and so many major attractions were built around this time.

In the 1930s, Southern Railways began a programme of mass electrification on their lines and one of their earliest flagship commissions was the Brighton Belle, an electric Pullman service which ran from London Victoria to Brighton. The train first ran in 1933 and continued to operate for nearly forty years. Its first-class coaches and steward service offered a level of luxury not usually seen on the mainline and attracted famous names, including Dora Bryan and Terence Rattigan, keen to enjoy the journey. Laurence Olivier travelled on the train regularly and famously complained to the Pullman Company when they dared to remove kippers from the breakfast menu; they were subsequently reinstated.

The area's importance to the entertainment industry was sealed in 1974, when the Brighton Dome hosted the Eurovision Song Contest. A little-known band called ABBA was introduced to sing Sweden's entry, a catchy little number called *Waterloo*. Despite the best efforts of the UK jury, who gave them 'Nil points', ABBA was victorious and the rest, as they say, is history. Olivia Newton-John, who represented the UK and came in a creditable 4th with *Long Live Love*, also went on to become a worldwide star, so it was definitely a year to remember.

The well-known author, Peter James was born in Brighton and uses the area as the setting for all of his award-winning crime novels featuring Detective Inspector Roy Grace. The books have been translated into over thirty languages and have sold more than twenty million copies worldwide. Since 2021, they have been adapted for an ongoing television series with actor, John Simm in the lead role.

Brighton and Hove were given joint city status in 2001 but still retain different identities and are seen by many as adjoining, but separate, settlements that sit near the border between East and West Sussex. Although the city is now a unitary authority with its own administration, it is within the ceremonial county of East Sussex. The only other city in Sussex is Chichester, which is thirty-five miles away in West Sussex.

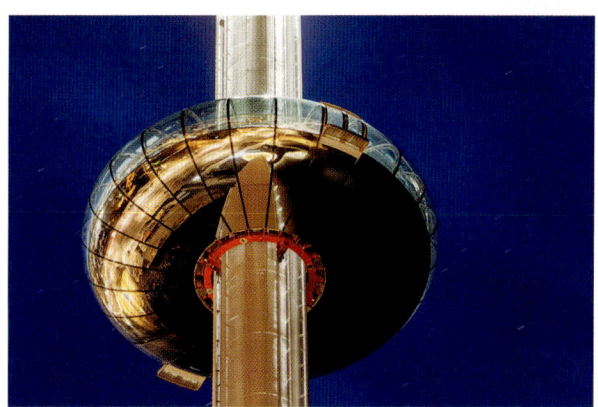

The seafront at Brighton is home to a number of iconic attractions; some that have been enjoyed by visitors since Victorian times and others a little newer. The most recent addition is the Brighton i360 *(left & above top)*, a moving observation tower that stands at the landward end of the skeletal remains of the historic West Pier *(above middle)*. Opened in 2016, the tower is 162 metres high. The viewing platform ascends and descends around the central column and can hold up to 200 people.

The Victorian bandstand *(above)* has a much longer history and first opened in 1884. It reopened following a major restoration project in 2009 and plays host to a variety of bands during the summer season. It can also be hired for weddings and other ceremonies.

Right: Brighton's West Pier was designed by Eugenius Birch and opened in 1866. After closing to the public in the 1970s, it gradually fell into disrepair and, following storms and two separate fires, only a metal framework remains.

Above: The Brighton Metropole is now a hotel and conference centre in the DoubleTree by Hilton group, but its history can be traced back to 1890. It was originally designed by Alfred Waterhouse, who was also the architect for the Natural History Museum in London. When completed, it was one of the largest hotels outside the capital and special trains were chartered to bring visitors down for the opening.

Below: The Regency Restaurant building on King's Road was once the home of Harriet Mellon, widow of banker Thomas Coutts, wife of the 9th Duke of St Albans and one of the richest women in Europe. The ground floor became a restaurant in the early 1930s and is one of the oldest in Brighton.

The Brighton Palace Pier (left & above) was the third pier to be built in Brighton but is the only one still in use. Officially opened in 1899, it was originally called the Brighton Marine Palace and was designed by Richard St George Moore. At more than 520 metres long, the pier presents an ongoing maintenance challenge, and a lot of hard work is needed to keep it in the best condition. Every year, the whole structure gets a new coat of paint, a job that takes three months to complete.

Brighton welcomes more than 9.5 million day visitors each year and although it can sometimes be hard to find a space on the shingle beach *(right)*, it is still possible to find quieter times *(above top)*. Palace Pier *(above)* is a good place to relax in the sun and take in the seafront views. Brighton beach faces south-west and stretches between the marina and the bandstand, a distance of over two and half miles.

Brighton Palace Pier and the seafront offer a wide range of attractions to entertain the huge numbers of people that visit each year. SEA LIFE Brighton *(p.143 bottom left)* is an aquarium that has been a feature of Marine Parade since it opened in 1872. The oldest operating aquarium in the world, it was designed by the architect, Eugenius Birch who had designed the West Pier a few years earlier. The aquarium is divided into various zones and visitors can experience a ride in a glass bottomed boat. There are more than five thousand creatures to see, and many different species are represented.

Above: Traditional carousel on Palace Pier.

P.143 – Top: Horror Hotel, Palace Pier. *Bottom middle:* Mr Punch puppet. *Bottom right:* Punch & Judy Show; Elvis Presley mannequin on seafront.

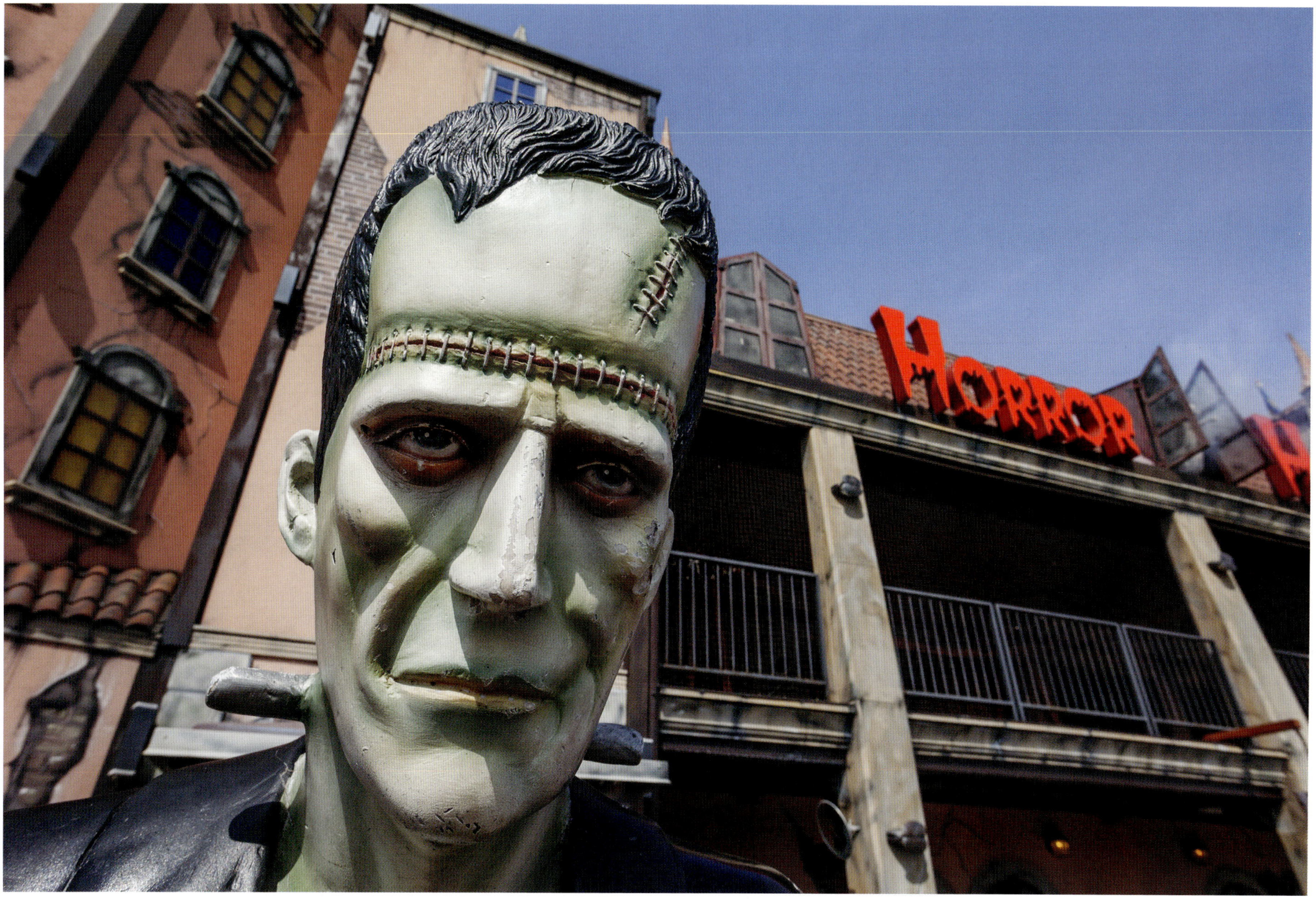
HORROR

PUNCH & JUDY

FISH & CHIPS

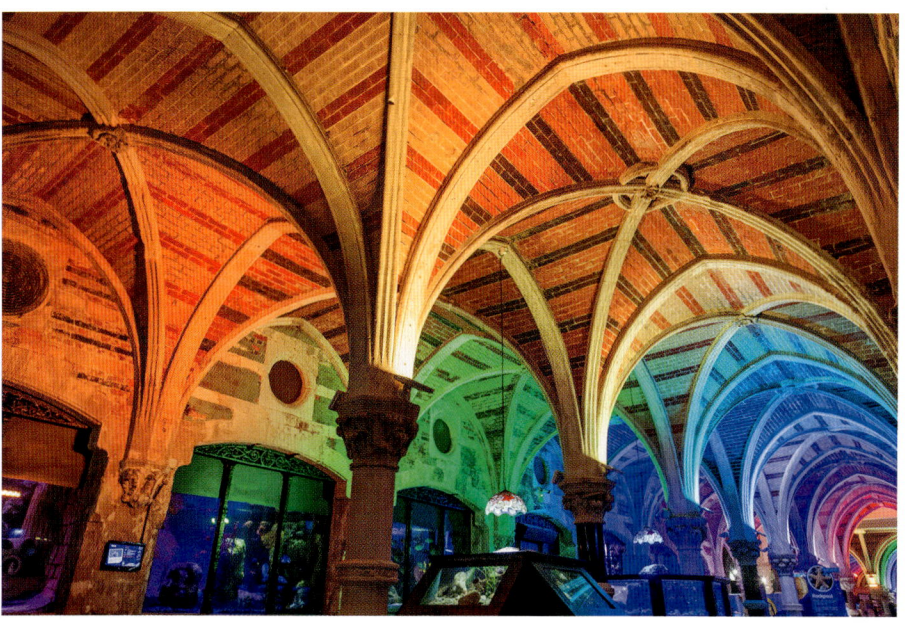

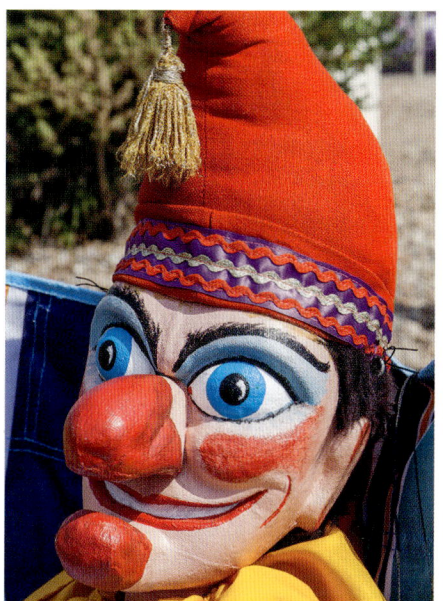

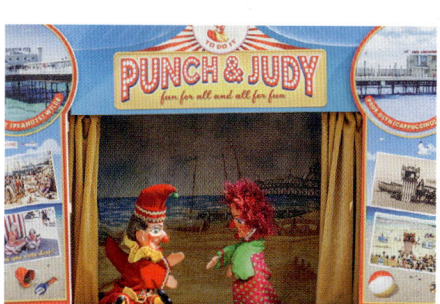

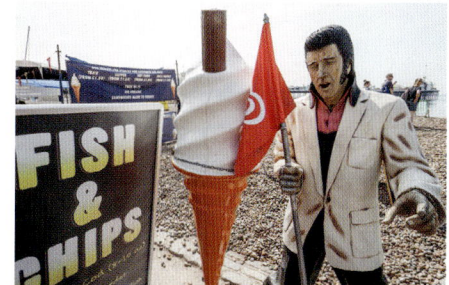

The Royal Pavilion at Brighton *(left)* was built as a seaside retreat and pleasure palace for the future King George IV when he was the Prince of Wales *(above)*. George first rented the pavilion in the 1780s, when it was still a modest lodging house. He commissioned Henry Holland to extend the building, but it wasn't until 1815 that the architect, John Nash was brought in to create the lavish spectacle seen today. Construction took several years and no expense was spared. George lived extravagantly and the Pavilion's Indo-Islamic exterior complemented his love of the exotic.

Above top: The North Gate (1832).

Brighton Pavilion was used as a military hospital during the First World War but, from 1920, an ongoing programme of restoration gradually returned the interiors to their former glory, with the latest project, the Saloon *(above middle)*, only being completed in 2018. Other lavish rooms include the Music Room *(left)* and Banqueting Room *(above top & bottom)*.

Prince George's presence in Brighton was very beneficial to the development of the town and population numbers increased from just over 3500 in 1786 to more than 40,000 by the 1820s.

Brighton has become known for its vibrant cultural and arts scene and is a mecca for shoppers. Mainstream stores are well represented, but it is the wide-ranging independent shops that are particularly appealing. The Lanes (*right & above*) are a famous part of the city, with a maze of streets full of quirky shops and restaurants. They were laid out in the late 18th century on what was part of the earlier settlement of Brighthelmstone. The narrow alleyways of The Lanes are known locally as twittens. One of the many hostelries serving refreshment is the historic Pump House, which was first recorded as a pub in 1776. The name is said to come from a pump house that used to pump seawater ashore for medicinal bathing in the 18th century.

Kemptown *(pp.150-151)* is an area of Brighton with its own distinct personality. It stretches from east of the city centre along to Brighton Marina and is known for its Regency terraces, set around seafront squares, although many of the grand buildings have since been converted into flats and bars. St George's Road and St James Street are home to a range of vintage stores, independent shops and cafes. Brighton is famous for its strong LGBTQ+ community. The Pride festival is held in the city every summer and Kemptown is at the centre of the celebrations.

Every August, on the first full weekend of the month, the streets of Brighton become a riot of colour, as the celebrated Pride festival takes place in the city. Its reputation as one of the best international Pride festivals is well-established and more than 300,000 people travel from around the world to join in the fun.

P.133: The Hove Pride Hut, Hove Lawns.

Pride promotes equality and diversity, and aims to stop all discrimination against the LGBTQ+ community. Brighton Pride gained in popularity in the 1990s, which led to an increase in support and sponsorship. It has been based at Preston Park to the north of the city centre since 1996. The Pride weekend brings an estimated boost of £22.5 million to Brighton's economy.

A number of different events take place at Brighton Pride and a traditional community parade is a central feature. Starting at Hove Lawns, the decorated floats travel along the seafront before heading north up London Road to Preston Park, which is the venue for the *Pride in the Park* concert. Headlining acts have included Britney Spears, Kylie Minogue and Mariah Carey. Other events include an arts festival and a dog show – and lots of parties.

Just east of Brighton, above the village of Rottingdean, is the striking silhouette of Beacon Mill *(left & above top)*, which can be seen for miles around. Built in 1802 to grind corn, this weatherboarded smock mill had fallen into disrepair by the early 20th century but underwent a series of repairs and renovations over the following decades and now opens to the public on certain days each summer. On the outskirts of Hove is West Blatchington windmill *(above)*, a hexagonal smock mill that sits on top of a flint tower above surrounding barns. Dating from the 1820s, its original workings are still in place. Demonstrations take place to show how corn is ground into flour and there is also a display of historical agricultural and milling items.

Eleven miles west of Brighton is the seaside town of Worthing, which is home to more than 110,000 people. The Latin motto on the town's crest is *Ex terra copiam e mari salute,* which means 'from the land fullness and from the sea health' when translated. Originally a small fishing village, Worthing became a fashionable resort in the 1750s and King George III's daughter, Amelia visited to recover her health in 1798.

An outdoor gallery called Art on the Pier was established on Worthing Pier in 2012 and the glass panels *(above)* provide a colourful backdrop for a range of exhibitions by established artists and young people.

Above top: Seafront guesthouses.

Right: Worthing beach looking to the pier.

Worthing Pier *(left & above)* was named 'Pier of the Year' in 2019 and provides a focus for the seafront. Designed by Sir Robert Rawlinson, it opened as a promenade deck in 1862. The buildings were added later and the one at the land end of the pier is home to the Pavilion Theatre and Atrium Bar. In the middle is an amusement arcade that dates from 1937. The Southern Pavilion at the far end is also an Art Deco gem and has recently been renovated. East of the pier on Marine Parade stands the Dome Cinema *(above top)*. Originally called the Kursaal, it was built as a leisure complex around 1910. Renamed during the First World War, it became a cinema in 1921 and is one of the oldest still operating in England.

Worthing's coastline is ideal for watersports, with windsurfing and kitesurfing being particularly popular. In 2009, two experienced local kitesurfers managed the terrifying feat of jumping over Worthing Pier. With winds gusts of over 40mph, the hazardous leap was not undertaken lightly. The village of Lancing adjoins the town and has shallow water that is perfect for beginners to the sport (pp164-165). The gently shelving beach means that those taking a tumble can just stand up and start again.

Littlehampton is a seaside resort at the mouth of the River Arun, twenty miles to the west of Brighton. Two beaches of sand and shingle are popular with visitors and attractions include the unusual East Beach Café *(above top)*, which was designed by the Heatherwick Studio and received recognition from the Royal Institute of British Architects in 2008. Littlehampton is also home to the longest bench in Britain *(left & above)*. The structure is 324 metres long and local school children helped Studio Weave with its design. Many of the wooden bench slats are engraved with messages from local people and visitors. *Below:* Dinky Doo Diner.

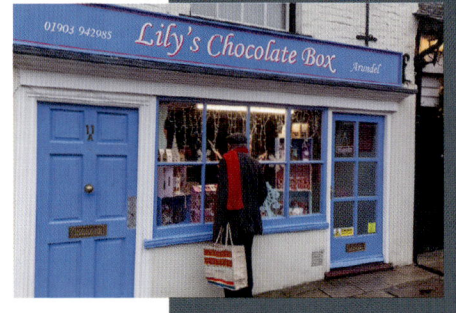

Following the course of the River Arun north from Littlehampton leads to Arundel, a market town whose fairytale castle dominates the skyline *(above)*. The town has a thriving arts scene, and an Open House Trail in August gives local artists and craftspeople the chance to turn their houses into temporary galleries. The annual Arundel Festival coincides with the trail and is a ten-day celebration of the arts that has been held for over forty-five years. Arundel has many independent shops *(left)* that attract shoppers throughout the year and a monthly local farmers' market. The High Street, Bond Street and Tarrant Street were used as locations for the 2024 film, *Wicked Little Letters*, starring Olivia Colman and Jessie Buckley. *PP.170-171:* Arundel Castle

There has been a castle at Arundel since the 11th century, when Roger de Montgomery built a motte and bailey castle in a commanding position overlooking the River Arun. The motte or mound, which rises over 100 feet above the dry moat below, dates from this period and is one of the oldest features left standing. The castle was largely rebuilt by Henry Fitzalan-Howard, the 15th Duke of Norfolk in the 19th century and became the Gothic masterpiece seen today. The castle has been the seat of the Dukes of Norfolk and their forebears for over 850 years. Every April, the gardens become a riot of colour as the annual Tulip Festival gets underway. More than 10,000 Red Oxford tulips cover the sloping castle banks *(left & p.173 top right)* and more than 120 different named tulips appear in displays throughout the grounds.

Other features of Arundel Castle that date from the 11th century are the Gatehouse, the Barbican and the impressive Keep *(above left)*, which stands on top of the motte. Visitors can climb the 131 steps to the Keep and enjoy fine views of the surrounding countryside from the top of the walls. The current Duke of Norfolk, Edward Fitzalan-Howard is also Earl Marshal, a title his family have held since 1672. Among the responsibilities attached to this is the organisation of major ceremonial state occasions, including the State Opening of Parliament, the Funeral of Queen Elizabeth II and the Coronation of King Charles III.

The State Rooms of Arundel Castle contain many treasures, and the luxurious interiors provide a dramatic contrast to the stone defences outside. Paintings by artists including Gainsborough, Canaletto and Van Dyck adorn the walls and there is also an important collection of 16th century furniture and Gobelin tapestries. Queen Victoria and Prince Albert visited the castle in 1846 and stayed in a suite of rooms *(p.174 left middle)* that were built specifically for them by the 13th Duke. The major renovations that took place between the 1870s and 1890s used the designs of Charles Alban Buckler and included the Grand Staircase *(p.174 bottom right)* and Dining Room *(right)*.

P.174 – Top left: The Drawing Room

Top right: Mary FitzAlan (1540-1557), wife of the 4th Duke of Norfolk; *Thomas Howard, 3rd Duke of Norfolk* (1473-1554) by Hans Holbein the Younger.

Bottom left: The Baron's Hall

The Fitzalan Chapel *(above & below)* sits within the grounds at Arundel Castle and was founded in 1380 by Richard Fitzalan, the 4th Earl of Arundel. It was damaged in the Civil War and later fell into disrepair but was restored in the 19th century and contains many tombs and monuments to the Fitzalan-Howard family *(left)*. Forty-eight of the misericords, or mercy seats, within the chapel are original; a few that had been damaged were replaced during the renovations. The chapel forms the chancel of the church of St Nicholas, which is very unusual as it is one of the few places of worship divided between the Roman Catholic and Anglican faiths.

Arundel Castle opens to visitors throughout the summer season and also offers a programme of popular special events. One of the highlights is the festival of International Medieval Jousting, which runs for six days around the end of July. The titans of the jousting world clash lances against shields, while galloping at high speeds, to decide who is the victor – although there is also a prize for the most chivalrous. The festival includes a whole range of themed displays and activities, including falconry, axe throwing and archery demonstrations, with medieval musicians adding to the atmosphere.

The gardens at Arundel Castle cover forty acres and offer a variety of landscapes that have been sympathetically developed to look beautiful and to provide a friendly environment for local wildlife. The Tulip Festival in April may be one of the highlights of the year but there are many others. The gardens include formal areas, such as the Collector Earl's garden *(right)*, which features green oak pagodas and water fountains, but also less formal, including an unusual Stumpery designed using old tree trunks. There are greenhouses full of exotic fruits and a Victorian vine and peach house *(above left)*, originally built in 1853 by Clarke & Hope.

Right & above top: The Tulip Festival. *Above right:* Arundel Castle in spring

Another of the seaside resorts in West Sussex is Bognor Regis, which grew rapidly after the coming of the railways in the 1860s. King George V stayed for three months in 1929 in an attempt to recover his health and, as a result, the suffix of 'Regis' was added to the town's name. Butlin's has been associated with Bognor since 1932, when Billy Butlin opened an amusement arcade on the Esplanade. More than ninety years later, Butlin's Bognor Regis can now accommodate 5,500 people on a 60-acre site that includes modern hotels and a conference centre. The Victorian Pier *(left)* opened in 1865 and was originally nearly three times longer than its current 107 metres.

Above: Bognor Rock Shop on The Esplanade. *Below:* Fishing boat being pulled out to sea.

PP.182-183: The beach at dawn, Bognor.

The only city in West Sussex is Chichester, which is home to around thirty-three thousand people. The settlement became established following the Roman invasion and large sections of today's city walls still date from this period. The remains of a Roman bath house were discovered during construction work in the 1960s and 1970s, and these are now preserved in The Novium, a museum that was built around them, which opened in 2012.

At the centre of the city is the Chichester Cross *(right & top left)*, an ornate market cross that was built in Perpendicular style. An inscription on the stonework suggests that this was built in the late 15th century by Edward Story, the Bishop of Chichester but it may be a little earlier. It is built of Caen stone and was used as a trading place until the early 19th century. A bust of King Charles I by Hubert Le Sueur stood in a niche on the Cross from the 1660s. It was later removed and replaced with a replica *(below left)*, but the original can be seen in The Novium.

Below right: Chichester street market.

Chichester Cathedral *(left & above top)* was founded in 1075 and has been at the heart of the community for 950 years. The building has been adapted, restored and extended over the centuries and so displays a number of architectural styles. The spire is amongst the tallest in England and can be seen for miles around. In 1861, the spire and central tower completely collapsed and a replica, which was slightly taller than the original, was then built by George Gilbert Scott. Cruciform in shape, the cathedral has an aisled nave and choir, crossed by a transept. The Lady chapel extends from the eastern end.

Above: The West Porch.

Chichester Cathedral suffered a fire in 1187. This destroyed much of the original Norman stonework and the timber-roofed nave, which was rebuilt in the 13th century. The arched Arundel Screen divides the quire from the nave *(left)*. It dates from the 15th century but was removed in 1859, revealing cracks that ultimately led to the collapse of the tower two years later. The screen was later reinstalled in its original position and dedicated in 1961. The High Altar is visible through the screen with its colourful backdrop, a tapestry by John Piper that dates from 1966.

In the north aisle is the Arundel Tomb *(left)*, topped by the recumbent figures of Richard Fitzalan, 3rd Earl of Arundel and his second wife, Eleanor of Lancaster. This notable Gothic tomb inspired a poem by Philip Larkin. The cathedral is home to the work of artists over the centuries, from the medieval to the modern. The Chagalle Window *(below)* was unveiled in 1978 and is a striking visual interpretation of Psalm 150, *Let everything that has breath praise the Lord.*

Right: Tower ceiling. *Below left:* Tudor painting of *Simon Sidenham* by Lambert Barnard, one of a set on display in the North Transept.

The Tangmere Military Aviation Museum is based at a former RAF station just to the east of Chichester. The collection includes many iconic aircraft and spans the period from the First World War to the Cold War. Displays pay particular reference to RAF Tangmere and the role that it played in history *(p.190 top & bottom left)*. The museum opened in 1982 and serves as a memorial to those who lost their lives in conflict and is staffed entirely by volunteers.

Left: Westland Lysander MkIII (SD). *Below:* McDonnell Douglas Phantom.

P.190 bottom right: Hawker Hunter Mk3 WB188.

Selsey is a seaside town that lies nine miles from Chichester. It is the most southerly town in Sussex and has a mix of sand and shingle beaches that are popular with water sports, walking and wildlife enthusiasts.

There has been an active Lifeboat Station at Selsey for over 160 years. In 2017, a new boathouse and visitor centre was built, with a shop, viewing gallery and a display area that provides information about the RNLI and tells the story of the station. The Shannon-class lifeboat, the *RNLI 13-20 Denise and Eric (above)* replaced the previous Tyne-class vessel in the same year. The lifeboat crew *(left)* are all volunteers.

Bosham is an attractive village on a small inlet of Chichester Harbour *(right)*. There has been a settlement here since Roman times and the Bosham Head, which is part of the largest Roman statue found in Britain, was unearthed here around 1800. The Holy Trinity Church *(above left)* is Grade I listed, and parts of the building are Saxon in origin.

Top: The Anchor Bleu by the harbour. *Above right:* The High Street.

Bosham (pronounced *Bozzum*) was one of the most important towns in Sussex during the Saxon period but is now a popular leisure destination. The tidal harbour is an unspoilt haven for wildlife. Many different bird species visit throughout the year, including whimbrel, dunlin and wigeon.

Two of England's important Roman sites are found in Sussex, at Fishbourne near Chichester and at Bignor to the north of Arundel. Fishbourne Roman Palace is the largest known residence in Britain that dates from the Roman period. It was built around AD 75, which is only thirty years after the Roman conquest of Britain began. A museum now covers the excavated remains that include the UK's largest collection of in situ mosaics *(above top)*.

Bignor Roman Villa was discovered in 1811 by George Tupper when he was out ploughing, and the site is still managed by the Tupper family today. The courtyard villa is renowned for the quality of its mosaic floors, which are amongst the best in the country. These include mosaics of Venus *(left)*, Medusa *(above)* and the Gladiators *(above middle)*.

LETTING OFF STEAM

Heading inland from the coastline, the landscape opens up and is dotted with attractive villages that are full of rural charm. Much of Sussex lies on the Wealden Anticline, and its geology is characterised by the bands of higher land that cross from west to east. The once-forested High Weald Area of Outstanding Natural Beauty and the Low Weald meet the rolling hills of the South Downs National Park. The highest point in the National Park is also the highest point in the county; this is Blackdown, which stands 280 metres above sea level.

Food has an important place in the county's history, with a range of delicacies that are as varied as the landscape. Traditional favourites evolved from ingredients that were available locally. An old folk poem quotes seven different dishes as 'good things' of Sussex, with Arundel mullet, and Amberley trout amongst the choices.

Sussex Pond Pudding is another classic dish from the region and was first recorded in the late 17th century. Made from suet pastry, this pudding is filled with butter and sugar before being steamed or boiled for several hours. A later development involved the adding of a whole lemon to the centre of the dish before cooking, which added a sharpness to offset the richness of the flavour.

More recently, the county has become known for its wines and cheeses. During World War II, rationing resulted in the virtual destruction of Britain's cheese industry. All cheesemakers were forced to produce the same product, which was known as Government Cheddar, and regional specialities disappeared. Recovery took a long time, but the British cheese industry is now one of the best in the world and produces over 750 different varieties. In Sussex, the High Weald Dairy in Haywards Heath crafts a range of artisan cheeses from cow, sheep and goat's milk and Sussex Charmer cheese is made by Bookham Harrison Farms in Rudgwick.

Sussex has a warm climate and soil similar to the Champagne region, which are both ideal for vineyards and wine production. In 2022, the term 'Sussex wine' was granted Protected Designation of Origin status, which means that it can only be applied to wine produced in the county. With around 140 vineyards, Sussex is one of the most important wine producers in England, accounting for nearly a third of the total. Many of the local towns, including Arundel, East Grinstead and Chichester, hold regular farmer's markets featuring the best seasonal produce.

The unofficial motto of Sussex is an expression in local dialect, We wunt be druv, which means that its inhabitants will not be pushed around and are independent of spirit. Literally, the phrase means We will not be driven and possibly the sole exception to this rule should be when you are in the safe hands of the train drivers at one of the county's most popular heritage attractions, the Bluebell Railway.

The village of South Harting (right) lies in the Chichester District of West Sussex and is typical of the attractive little settlements dotted across the Sussex downland landscape. It has a population of just over eight hundred, which supports two churches, a primary school and a country inn called The White Hart. The Church of St Mary and St Gabriel (above top) is the parish church and stands at the southern end of the village. It mainly dates from the 14th century, although there are signs of earlier work. It was significantly restored following a fire in the 16th century. Statues within the church include the Archangel Gabriel (above) by Philip Jackson which hangs in the North transept. The First World War memorial in the churchyard was designed by Eric Gill.

Just on the edge of South Harting, and enjoying an elevated position on the South Downs, is Uppark *(below)*, a 17th century house that is in the care of the National Trust. It was originally built for Ford Grey, the Earl of Tankerville, in 1690. However, it was the ownership of Sir Matthew Fetherstonhaugh in the 18th century that resulted in the fine Georgian interiors and extensive collection of art and furniture seen today. He bought Uppark in 1747 and commissioned the architect, James Paine to redesign the interiors. Sir Matthew and his wife travelled Europe, collecting paintings and objects *(left & bottom)* to complement the new spaces, some of which were created especially for them.

Every Autumn, the fields at Rogate Pumpkin Patch turn a distinctive shade of orange as the annual crop of pumpkins ripen in the sun. Found half-way between Midhurst and Petersfield, Slade Farm holds a series of family events each October, with plenty of pumpkin-themed activities, including spooky games that are perfect for Halloween.

The country town of Midhurst *(p.205)* sits by the River Rother in West Sussex. The heritage of the town is notable, with more than ninety listed buildings in a variety of architectural styles, including examples from the Tudor, Georgian, Victorian and Edwardian periods. The centre of the Old Town is the Market Square, where the surrounding buildings are primarily Tudor in origin. The Spread Eagle Hotel on South Street *(right)*, which was originally a coaching inn, dates from the 15th century.

The atmospheric Cowdray Heritage Ruins stand within Cowdray Park, to the east of Midhurst. Although there had been a fortified manor on the site since the 13th century, Cowdray House was built in the 1520s and became one of England's great Tudor houses. Over the following decades, it received a number of important royal visitors, including Henry VIII, Edward VI and Elizabeth I. A major fire in 1793 largely destroyed the house, but the ruins are still of great significance and are Grade I listed.

The Weald and Downland Living Museum is an independent, open-air museum that rescues and conserves historic buildings. Founded in 1970, the seventy-acre site is home to over fifty buildings that span a time period of nearly 900 years. The original aim of the museum was to rescue buildings from across South East England that were threatened with destruction and had an architectural significance reflecting local traditions and practice. The museum is committed to the idea of lifelong learning. Thousands of school children visit each year and an ongoing series of courses and workshops for adults focus on traditional crafts and trades

The magnificent country house of Petworth *(left)* dates from the late 17th century and is Grade I listed. Inspired by European palaces, such as Versailles, it was built for the 6th Duke of Somerset and his wife, Lady Elizabeth Percy, who was a great heiress. She brought a number of large estates to the marriage, of which Petworth was one. Since 1750, the house has been owned by the Wyndham family and it was Charles Wyndham, the 2nd Earl of Egremont who commissioned Lancelot 'Capability' Brown to landscape the parkland in the mid-18th century. Although the house and grounds were handed to the nation in 1947 and are cared for by the National Trust, the current Lord and Lady Egremont continue to live in the house, as their forebears have for over two hundred and seventy years.

Above top: Rotunda in Petworth Park. *Above left:* Grand Staircase with murals by Louis Laguerre. *Above right:* Portrait of Henry VIII from Hans Holbein's studio, with frame by Grinling Gibbons.

Petworth is home to one of the finest art collections cared for by the National Trust. Although some important pieces had been collected by previous owners, it was George Wyndham, the 3rd Earl of Egremont, who expanded the collection and became patron to artists of the day, including JMW Turner and John Constable. Inheriting the house in 1763, he enlarged the North Gallery *(above)*, which had been built by his father to display classical sculptures, to ensure his more contemporary art could be displayed to best advantage. George Wyndham's tenure has since become known as the 'Golden Age' of Petworth.

Right: The Creation of Pandora by Louis Laguerre, Grand Staircase ceiling.

Sussex is a county known for its quaint local pubs, many of which are surrounded by beautiful countryside, ideal for walkers and cyclists. The George & Dragon is in the village of Houghton, just west of Amberley and alongside the River Arun. One of the oldest pubs in Sussex, it is believed to pre-date the English Civil War and has a large inglenook fireplace, ideal for cosy winter evenings. In the summer, visitors can relax in the garden and enjoy views across the South Downs National Park

The village of Amberley is home to Amberley Museum, an open-air industrial heritage museum that occupies a thirty-six acre site next to the railway station. Opening to the public in 1979, the museum was the idea of a group of like-minded individuals, including architects, surveyors and planners, who wanted to create a space where the industrial and social history of South East England could be conserved within an active working environment, so that future generations could experience, understand and learn from the past. Over the following decades, the museum has continued to add to its collections and also offers a range of demonstrations and exhibitions. A few of the many buildings now on site are a signal box, rural telephone exchange, timber yard with steam crane and a fire station *(right)*.

Above: Reconstructed village garage & car repair shop from the 1930s.

One of the buildings at Amberley Museum is a reconstructed Southdown Bus Garage, which dates from the 1920s. This houses a number of working vintage buses, which are mainly from Southdown Motor Services and have distinctive green livery *(above)*. Bus rides are available on museum open days.

P.217 - *Top left:* Simple Cell (battery). *Top right:* Display of vintage tools. *Bottom left:* Pottery demonstration. *Bottom right:* Blacksmith's shop.

To the north-west of Haywards Heath, in the village of Handcross, are the intriguing ruins, gardens and house of Nymans. Ludwig Messel bought Nymans in 1890 and began the work needed to create a home perfect for family life and for entertainment. Ludwig's eldest son, Leonard, inherited the house in 1915 and, encouraged by his wife Maud, undertook a complete redesign, transforming it into a mock medieval manor. He also continued his father's work on developing Nymans plant collections with head gardener, James Comber. Rare plants were sourced from regions as far afield as the Andes and Tasmania. In 1947, the house was largely destroyed by fire. It was partly rebuilt but the rest became a picturesque ruin *(left)* that forms a feature within the gardens *(above)*. Nymans was gifted to the National Trust in 1953 and continues to attract garden lovers from around the world.

ck Colonel Loses His Home on His 75th Birthday

Fire Destroys Famous
Sussex Mansion

VALUABLE ART GEMS LOST

Evening News Reporter

YMANS, Handcross, one of the most beautiful mansion

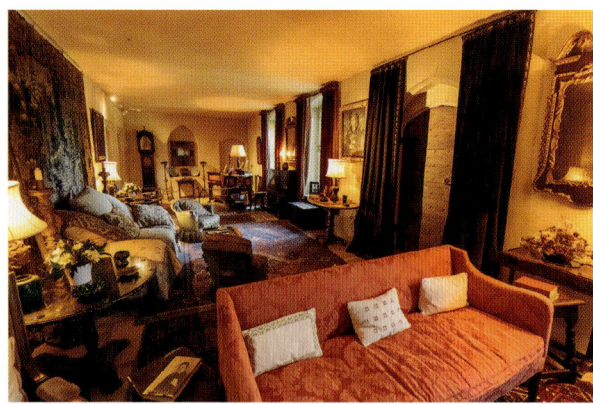

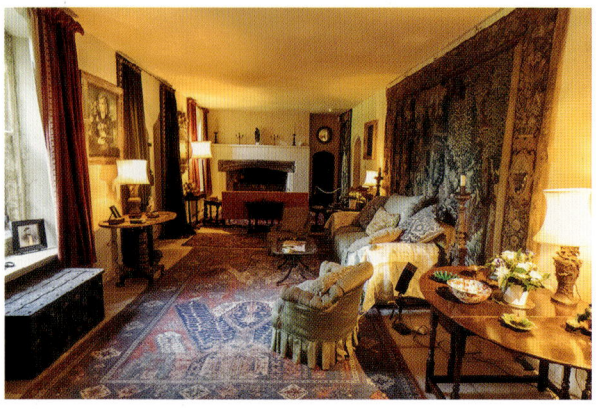

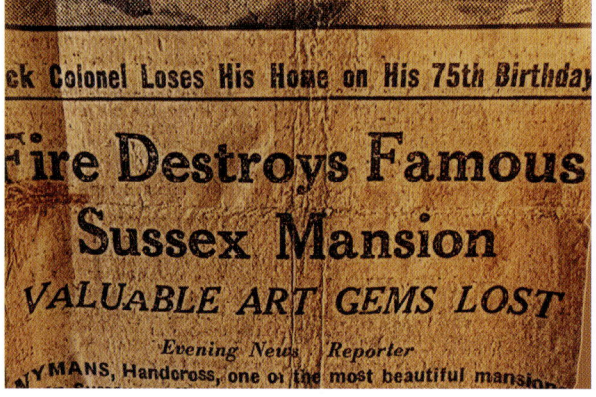

When fire ravaged the house at Nymans in 1947 *(above)*, it was still in the hands of the Messel family. Much of the house was damaged beyond repair but a section was made safe and became a base for Leonard's daughter, Anne and her husband, the 6th Earl of Rosse, when visiting the gardens. Anne later moved back permanently at the end of the 1970s and stayed until 1992. She was keen to preserve the intimate and charming feel of her parent's home and rooms are furnished with tapestries, furniture and art from their collection *(right & above)*. Anne's brother, Oliver, was a famous theatre designer and some of his paintings are on display.

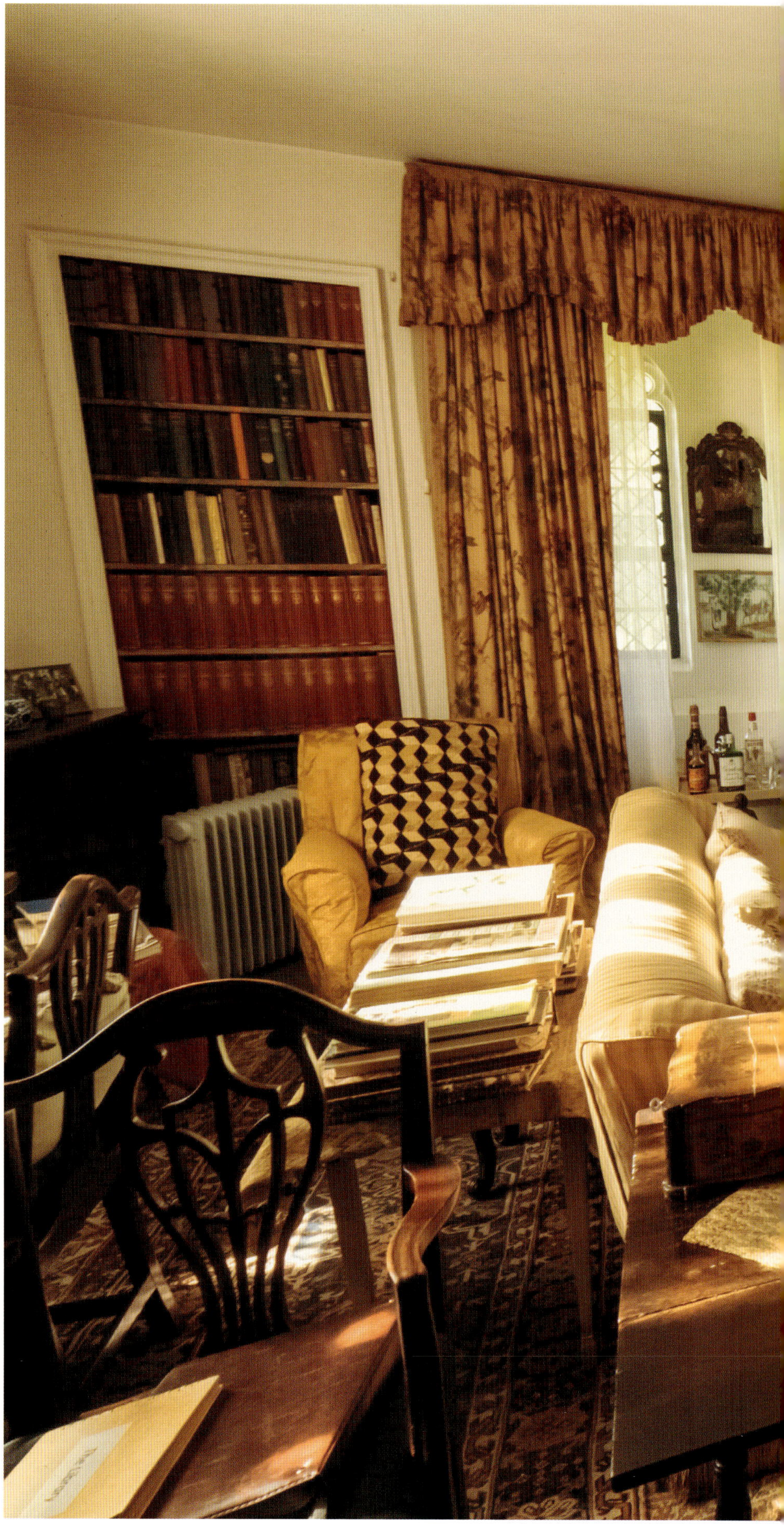

The Ouse Valley Viaduct (right) is an architectural marvel that was built to carry the London to Brighton railway line (above top). Construction began in 1839 and the elegant design consists of thirty-seven identical arches supported on red brick piers. The contract to build the viaduct offered a payment of £38,500, equal to £3.3 million today. The distinctive oval holes in the piers reduced the number of bricks required, but also create an interesting visual illusion (above), which attracts visitors today. Opened in 1841, the viaduct underwent major restoration in the 1890s and 1990s but has been protected by Grade II* listed status since 1983.

Wakehurst *(left & above right)* is a house and garden in the High Weald of West Sussex. Although owned by the National Trust, it is managed by the Royal Botanic Gardens Kew and is home to Kew's Millennium Seed Bank. The gardens cover five hundred acres and are home to a vast range of exotic trees and woodland plants, which have been planted to complement the natural landscape. Wakehurst has what is called a living plant collection, which sets it apart from many other public gardens. Plants are grown specifically for research, education, conservation or display; all are accurately identified and documented. The Millennium Seed Bank Partnership *(top & above left)* at Wakehurst guards against the future extinction of plants in the wild by storing seeds in underground vaults.

The ancient market town of East Grinstead sits on the northern boundary of the High Weald Area of Outstanding Natural Beauty. It is a hill town, built on a sandstone ridge, whose name derives from the Old English, *grenestede*, meaning 'green place'. The historic High Street has an impressive run of timber buildings that date from the 14th and 15th centuries. East Grinstead's position on a major route from London was key to its economic development and coaching inns were established to provide refreshment for weary travellers. By the end of the 18th century, the Crown *(right)* and the Dorset Arms *(above)* were the most important of these. The owner of The Dorset Arms established his own stagecoach service, running from London via East Grinstead and on to Brighton, in 1756.

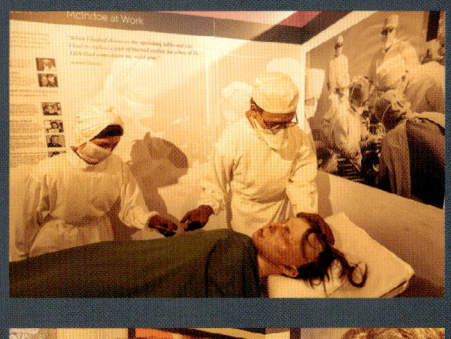

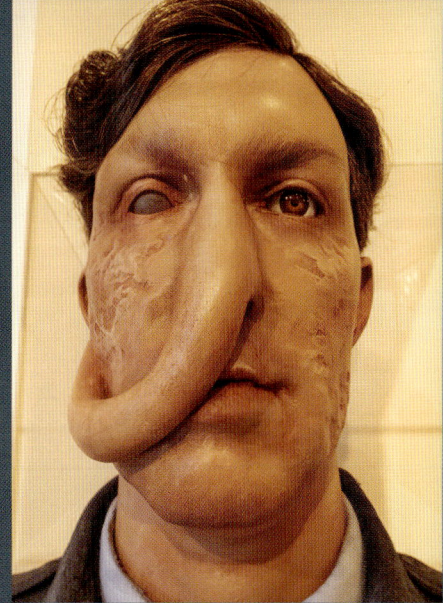

East Grinstead Museum has a collection of over 20,000 items that represent and interpret the heritage of the town and surrounding villages. One of the many interesting stories that it tells is that of Archibald McIndoe *(top right)*. He was a civilian plastic surgeon for the Royal Air Force and arrived at East Grinstead Hospital in 1939. He pioneered new ways of treating airmen recovering from severe burns *(above top)*. His patients went on to form The Guinea Pig Club, whose membership was open to Allied Aircrew who had undergone at least two operations at the hospital for crash related burns or other injuries; the doctors and surgeons who had treated them and also members of the Royal Society of Prevention of Cruelty to Guinea Pigs. The town of East Grinstead took the men to their hearts and went out of their way to make them feel included and welcome.

Left: High Street. *Above:* Judges Terrace.

Just to the south of East Grinstead is Standen, a house and garden in the Arts and Crafts style that is now cared for by the National Trust. The house *(above top)* was built as a comfortable family home and rural retreat for James and Margaret Beale and their family in the 1890s. It was designed by possibly the foremost architect of the Arts and Crafts Movement, Philip Webb. He was a friend of William Morris, and the fabrics and wallpapers at Standen were supplied by Morris & Co *(above & right)*. The house is now dressed as it would have appeared to guests visiting in 1925. Margaret Beale was a self-taught gardener but was inspired by Arts and Crafts principles and followed them to create the gardens at Standen, which cover twelve acres.

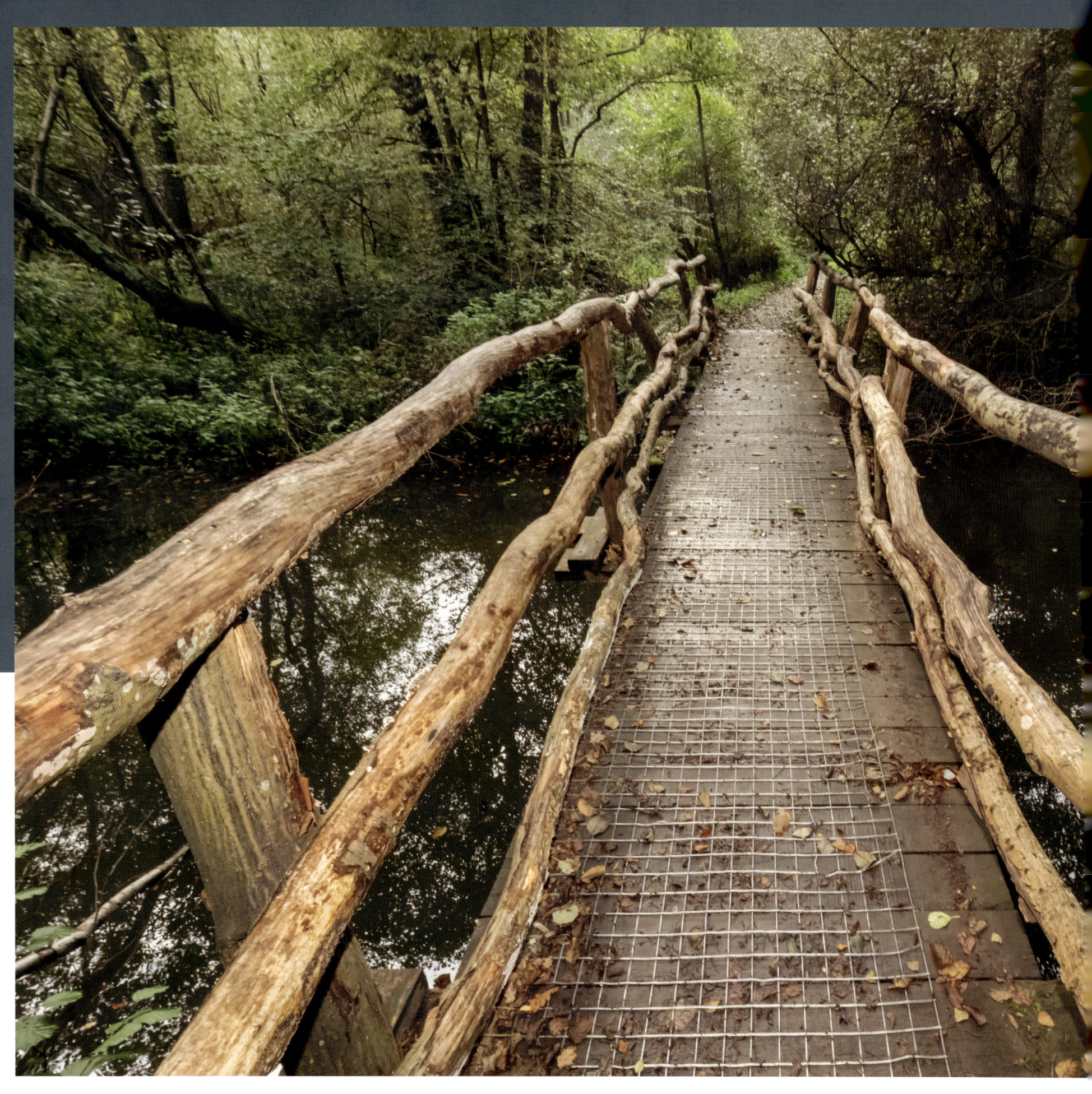

Sussex is a haven for horticultural enthusiasts and just ten miles south of Standen are the scenic, informal gardens of Sheffield Park. The gardens are a result of centuries of landscape design and owe much to Lancelot 'Capability' Brown who laid them out in the 1770s. Of the five lakes seen today, he created the Upper and Lower Woman's Way Pond. Humphrey Repton later completed further work at the end of the 18th century. Today, Sheffield Park is Grade I listed, and visitors are drawn to the ever-changing foliage of the many different tree species from all over the world. The National Trust has looked for ways to sympathetically revitalise areas of the garden and are currently working with two-time RHS Chelsea award-winner, Joe Perkins, to create a 120-acre planted oasis, which will be the first major renovation project they have undertaken since the gardens came into their care.

The Bluebell Railway is a heritage railway line that runs through eleven miles of beautiful countryside in the Sussex Weald near to Ashdown Forest. The route goes from Sheffield Park *(right)* to East Grinstead, with intermediate stops at Horsted Keynes *(above)* and Kingscote. Although the engines are capable of faster speeds, they travel at a maximum of 25 miles an hour on the largely single-track line.

P.198: Horsted Keynes station.

P.199: Signal box levers in the museum at Sheffield Park station.

The British Railways-operated line closed in the late 1950s and just one year later, a group of enthusiasts met and formed the Bluebell Railway Preservation Society. Their original plan was to re-open the whole line from East Grinstead to Culver Junction near Lewes, and to run it as a commercial service, but it was soon decided to focus on the section of track between Sheffield Park and Horsted Keynes and open it as a tourist route. The first train ran in the summer of 1960.

Left: SER 0-6-0 goods engine No. 65 at Sheffield Park.

Above from top: LBSCR Stroudley Terrier, No. 55 'Stepney' at Sheffield Park station; Horsted Keynes station; Signal box at Sheffield Park.

The Bluebell Railway now has one of the biggest collections of engines and rolling stock in the country, with over thirty locomotives and more than 160 carriages and wagons, many of which predate the Second World War. Largely managed and run by volunteers, the railway runs a number of special events throughout the year in addition to its scheduled timetable. Events include Santa Specials *(left)*, Silver service dining, Family fun days and Rail ale evenings. Other attractions provided along the route include the SteamWorks! interactive display at Sheffield Park and the Carriage and Wagon viewing gallery at Horsted Keynes.

Top left: Horsted Keynes station. *Top right:* Passengers in Victorian costume at Sheffield Park. *Bottom left:* Sheffield Park ticket office. *Bottom right:* Buffet at Horsted Keynes station.